Lyrical
Life Science

Volume 2
Mammals, Ecology, and Biomes

**Text and Lyrics by
Doug and Dorry Eldon**

**Performed by
Bobby Horton**

**Illustrations by
Eric Altendorf**

Published by:
Lyrical Learning
8008 Cardwell Hill
Corvallis, Oregon 97330
Telephone (541) 754-3579

This book and cassette tape set can be used by students of all ages. Young elementary students will benefit by becoming familiar with scientific terms through casual listening. Middle school students often study life science in sixth grade; the text and musical arrangements are intended for this age and older students. The information covered in the songs and text should be very familiar to high school students as they study biology in greater depth.

A workbook is also available. Ideally, these resources should be used in addition to hands-on activities where observation and application can be made. In this way, knowledge learned through reading and singing can become known through experience as well.

Cover art and design: Susan Moore
Illustrations: Eric Altendorf
Layout and design: Dorry Eldon
Sheet music layout: Lois Marie Zaerr
Scientific advisor: Dr. Karen Timm

Special thanks to: Dr. Karen Timm, Loverna Wilson,
Roberta Sobotka, Anne Hetherington

Illustrations redrawn with permission from:
Merlin D. Tuttle, Bat Conservation International
Spotted bat, false vampire bat, Franquet's flying fox, pocketed free-tailed bat

Nowak, Ronald M. and Paradiso, John L. *Walker's Mammals of the World 4th Edition,* Johns Hopkins University Press, Baltimore and London, 1983. Echidna, mouse deer, slender loris, galago, mouse lemur, sifaka, indri, aye aye, tarsier, emperor tamarin, and Goeldi's marmoset.

Photographic collection of Dr. Karen Timm
Giraffe with young, opossum, coyote, seal, sea lion, multi-sized horses, zebra, donkey laden with tortoise food, tapir, hippopotamus, llama, elk, antelope, long-horn, sheep, sheep on goat, guinea pig with doctor, rat, colobus monkey, hamster, chinchilla, capybara, tree shrew, orca, baboon and African elephant.

ISBN 0-9646367-2-7

TABLE OF CONTENTS

Introduction   2
List of Illustrations   3

Chapter 1   **Mammals**   4
                   Characteristics and classification

Chapter 2   **Monotremes and Marsupials**   8
                   Pouched and Egg-laying Mammals

Chapter 3   **Carnivores and Pinnipeds**   16
                   Meat-eating Mammals

Chapter 4   **Ungulates**   24
                   Odd- and Even-Toed Hoofed Mammals

Chapter 5   **Primates**   36

Chapter 6   **Rodents**   42
                   Gnawing Mammals

Chapter 7   **Rodent-like Mammals**   48
                   Lagomorphs: Pikas, Rabbits and Hares

Chapter 8   **Bats**   52
                   Chiroptera—Flying Mammals

Chapter 9   **Insectivores**   56
                   Insect-eating Mammals

Chapter 10   **"Toothless" Mammals**   60
                   Edentates: Armadillos, Anteaters, and Sloths

Chapter 11   **Whales**   64
                   Cetaceans: Baleen and Toothed Whales

Chapter 12   **Sirenians**   68
                   Sea Cows, Dugongs, Manatees

Chapter 13   **Single-Family Orders**   72
                   Elephant
                   Pangolin or Scaly anteater
                   Aardvark
                   Flying Lemur
                   Hyrax
                   Elephant shrew
                   Tree shrew

Chapter 14   **Ecology**   78

Chapter 15   **Biomes**   86

Appendix   Lyric Sheets   97
                   Notes/More Information
Bibliography
Index

INTRODUCTION

Welcome to *Lyrical Life Science Volume 2*. In this singing science text you will learn about the orders of mammals, ecology and biomes. Scientific vocabulary and a systematic classification system to organize information help scientists share their scientific knowledge. You'll be learning these two important factors of life science as you sing along to old-time tunes.

You may know most of the melodies on the accompanying cassette tape from summer camp, music class, your family or friends in the neighborhood. These are tunes that were popular in their heyday and have been passed down from generation to generation. A few of these "oldies" may not be familiar but were hits in their time. Some of these, such as "Kingdom Coming," were million-sellers!—Not as CDs, cassette tapes, or even records but as sheet music for sing alongs. Another hit, "Abraham's Daughters," was composed by a famous songwriter who also penned "Oh Where, Oh Where Has My Little Dog Gone."

America is not only full of toe-tapping tunes, but also many musical styles from cowboy lullabies to Irish jigs brought over by early immigrants. We've incorporated a number of these and other popular styles to give you a deeper knowledge and appreciation of America's musical past.

These old tunes form the basis for learning life science information. We all easily remember information put to familiar melodies (many adults still admit to using "Twinkle Twinkle Little Star" when they are alphabetizing). Researchers have conducted several studies that validate this type of musical learning (see introduction to *Lyrical Life Science Volume 1*). We think you, too, will remember scientific information after learning the songs in *Lyrical Life Science Volume 2*.

In *Lyrical Life Science Volume 1*, the five kingdoms of living things were studied — animal, plant, protist, fungi and monera, along with the scientific method and a summary of characteristics of all living things. *Lyrical Life Science Volume 2* is a continuation of this life science study.

There is a lot to learn, but with a sense of humor and fun toe-tapping music we think you're in for some good-time fun— and learning!

ILLUSTRATIONS

Aardvark	75	Hamster	46	Pronghorn	33
Aardwolf	19	Hare	50	Pygmy shrew	58
Aye aye	39	Hedgehog	57	Rabbit	50
Anteater	62	Hippopotamus	30	Raccoon	18
Antelope	34	Hoof, deer	28	Rainforest	92
Armadillo	61–62	horse	25	Rat	46
Baboon	40	rhino	25	Rhinoceros	28
Badger	19	Horse	25	Savanna	90
Baleen	66	Horses, all sizes	26	Sea Lion	23
Bats	53–45	Hyena	19	Sea Otter	19
Bear, grizzly	18	Hyrax	76	Seal	22
Beaver	45	Indri	38	Sheep	35
Biomes	87–95	Jaw, bear	18	Sifaka	38
Bison	34	beaver	43	Sloth	63
Blubber	65	deer	6	Soil	87
Donkey or Ass	26, 27	pinniped	17	Solenodon	58
Camel, bactrian	31	shrew	6	Spiny Anteater	15
dromedary	30	walrus	21	Squirrel	44
Capybara	47	whale	6	Stomach	31
Carbon/oxygen cycle	85	wolf	17	Tamarin, emperor	39
Cat, domestic	20	Kangaroo and joey	9	Tapir	27
Cheetah	20	Kangaroo, tree	9	Tarsier	39
Chimpanzee	41	Koala	11	Teeth, dolphin	67
Chinchilla	47	Lemur, mouse	38	porpoise	67
Chipmunk	44	ring-tailed	38	seal, crabeater	22
Coniferous forest	79, 91	Llama	31	Tenrec	59
Coyote	18	Lion	17	Tiger	20
Deer	79	Longhorn steer	33	Tree shrew	77
Deciduous forest	91	Loris	37	Tundra	88
Desert	88	Manatee	69–71	Vertebrae	5
Duck-billed platypus	14	Marine biome	95	Walrus	21
Dugong	69	Marmoset, Goeldi's	40	Warthog	29
Echidna	15	Marmot, woodchuck	44	Water cycle	83–84
Echolocation diagram	54	Mole	59	Whale, gray	66
Elephant	73	Mongoose	19	sperm	67
Elephant shrew	76	Mouse	46	Wolf	18
Elk	32	Mouse deer, chevrotain	32	Wombat	11
Flying lemur	75	Nitrogen cycle	85	Zebra	27
Food chain	82	Opossum	12		
Food web	83	Owl	80		
Freshwater biome	94	Pangolin	74		
Fur	20	Pika, conies	49		
Galago	37	Placenta with young	6		
Gibbon	41	Platypus	14		
Giraffe	32	Platypus, feet	14		
Giraffe and young	5	Porcupine	47		
Goat	25, 35	Prairie dog	43		
Grassland	89	Prehensile tail	37		
Hair follicle	5	Primate hands, feet	37		

MAMMALS
(to the tune of "Marines' Hymn")

Marines' Hymn is the anthem for the United States Marine Corps but the tune was adapted from an operetta by Offenbach, performed in France in 1859. Sometime later, new words were added by an unknown author—probably a marine.

Unknown   Lyrics by Doug and Dorry Eldon

There are nineteen orders of placental mammals in this class
You can learn of them in other songs but they're listed here real fast
They are grouped by how and what they eat, how they move or their features
Or where and how they live help to classify diverse creatures

There are rodents and the rodent-like, insect-eaters and flying bats
Carnivores and those without real teeth and the trunk-nosed elephants
There are many kinds with hoofs and there are water dwellers too
Primates you will remember for the order includes you

Mammals that walk and live on the land are all terrestrial
And the kinds that live up in the trees are all arboreal
Mammals that live in saltwater seas are what we call marine
There are also those that fly so high or can glide from tree to tree

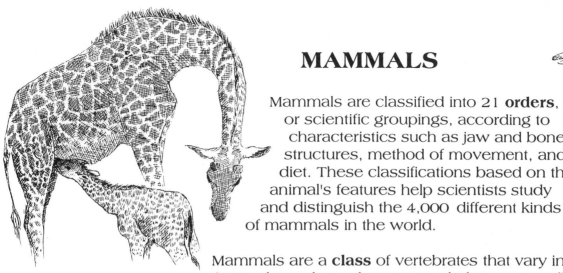

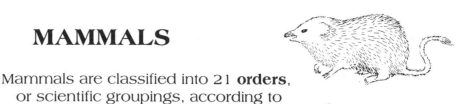

MAMMALS

Mammals are classified into 21 **orders**, or scientific groupings, according to characteristics such as jaw and bone structures, method of movement, and diet. These classifications based on the animal's features help scientists study and distinguish the 4,000 different kinds of mammals in the world.

The smallest land mammal is the pygmy shrew, shown actual size. The largest land mammal is the elephant whose eye alone is about the size of this shrew!

Mammals nurse their young with milk made in the mother's body.

Mammals are a **class** of vertebrates that vary in size and may be as large as a whale or as small as a pygmy shrew. Even with all their differences, mammals share several characteristics that separate, or distinguish them from other classes of animals such as fish, birds or reptiles. Mammals share the following features:

1- Mammary glands in the mother produce milk to feed the young. "Mamma" and "mammal" come from the same word.

2- Warmblooded or **endothermic**, means mammals' body temperatures are not regulated by outside temperatures, but stay about the same (97–102 degrees) no matter where they are. (Animals such as fish and frogs are coldblooded, or **ectothermic** which means their body temperatures are controlled by, and are the same as, temperatures outside their bodies.)

Backbone or vertebrae

3- Vertebrae, which form the **backbone**, are not unique to mammals but all mammals have them. They provide support for the skeletal system. The skeleton provides structure for tissues such as muscles, and protection for internal organs.

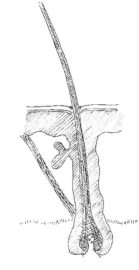

Hair grows from tiny pits in the skin called follicles. Most mammals have two kinds of hair: soft underfur for insulation and longer guard hairs for camouflage or protection.

4- Young are born alive to all mammals except monotremes, which hatch their young from eggs.

5- Hair, also called **pelage**, insulates mammals from temperature extremes, helping to keep their body temperatures the same. Whales and other marine mammals that have very little hair, have blubber, instead, for protection from the cold.

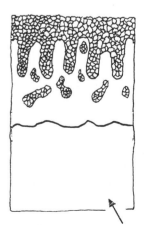

A thick layer of **blubber**, or fat, insulates several marine mammals.

REPRODUCTION

Mammals are also divided according to how they reproduce. In most mammals, 19 of the 21 orders, the young have fully developed in the **placenta** by birth.

The placenta is a structure inside the female through which the developing young receive food and oxygen. In **placental mammals**, the young are well developed when born. In **pouched mammals** the young are only partially developed when born. They crawl to and live in a pouch—a type of external placenta, to be protected and nourished until they are further developed. In the rare order of **egg-laying mammals**, the young hatch from eggs and continue to be nested by their mothers until they grow larger.

Young in placenta

CLASSIFICATION

After a mammal is classified into a particular order, it is further classified into a **family**. Its various features continue to separate it into a **genus** and then finally a **species**, which is the individual kind of mammal. With this classification system, scientists can categorize, study and compare various types of mammals.

Kingdom :   Animal
Phylum: Vertebrata
Class: Mammal
Order: Carnivora
Family: Canidae
Genus: Canus
Species: lupus

Scientific name: *Canus lupus*
Common name: Gray wolf

JAW STRUCTURES AND TEETH

Though mammals eat a wide variety of plants and animals, they are all **consumers** (as opposed to plants which are **producers**). The jaws and teeth are specialized, depending on their diet. This classifies them into one of three types of eaters.

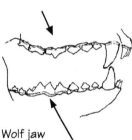

Wolf jaw
Large carnassials
shear meat.

1- Carnivores, or meat-eaters, have teeth that may include: **incisors** (front teeth); large **canine** (or dog teeth) for catching and holding their prey; **premolars** and **molars** (cheek teeth) for cutting or tearing meat, which include **carnassials** for shearing meat. An insectivorous diet (of insects) is also considered a type of carnivorous diet.

2- Herbivores, or plant-eaters, have teeth that may include: incisors with some specialized for gnawing, canines, and cheek teeth shaped for grinding plant material.

3- Omnivores, or anything-eaters, have teeth that may include incisors, canines, and cheek teeth for chewing.

Deer jaw
Predominant teeth
are grinding teeth

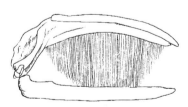

Baleen whale jaw
Baleen strains tiny
organisms from water
in the whale's mouth .

Shrew jaw
Insectivores eat
insects and worms.

Some mammals may not even have teeth, such as the anteater, but this lack suits them quite well. They have special enzymes to digest their food. Some whales have baleen instead of teeth to strain large amounts of water to collect the tiny organisms they need. A mammal's teeth or lack of them, is always dependent upon its diet.

LOCOMOTION

Mammals may live on land, in trees, in the air or in water. Their body structures show not only where they live, but how they move, or their means of **loco-motion**.

Most mammals are **quadrupeds** or **tetrapods** because they move on four feet. "Quad" and "tetra" mean four and "ped" or "pod" means feet.

Terrestrial mammals live on land and have features for walking or running. Some are **cursorial** with strong, long legs—features especially good for running to escape from being eaten.

Arboreal mammals live in trees and have arms and legs especially helpful for moving among branches. If they move through trees with an arm-swinging motion, like gibbons, they are called **brachiators**. Not all tree dwellers swing through trees; others, such as tarsiers, are **clinger-leapers**, that literally leap and cling from branch to branch.

Aquatic or **marine** mammals such as whales, manatees, seals and sea lions have features especially suited for water movement. Their fins, flippers and tails help them swim and navigate.

There is only one order of mammals that can actually **fly**—the bats. But there are others such as the flying lemur and flying squirrel that can glide among the tree tops.

There is a tremendous variety of species in the class of mammals—they come in all shapes and sizes and live in a variety of places. In the following chapters we will look closely at the 21 mammal orders. Later, we will study their relationships, interactions and the climatic regions where they live.

MONOTREMES and MARSUPIALS
(to the tune of "Aura Lea")

Aura Lea is a sentimental love song that was popular with Northern soldiers during the Civil War. It was revived and the tune used again for the love song: "Love Me Tender."

G. R. Poulton

Lyrics by Dorry Eldon

Ko - a - la, wom - bat, kang - a - roo and the wal - la - by they are pouched mar - su - pi - als there's six - teen fam - i - lies.

Chorus
Mon - o - tremes, mar - su - pi - als most live in Aus - tra - lia But the o - pos - sums have a pouch and live in A - mer - i - ca.

The young is born quite immature, it crawls to the pouch
It develops there within, before it comes out
Chorus

Many are herbivores, others carnivores
There's also insectivores, opossums are omnivores
Chorus

The two egg-laying monotremes live near Australia
There's the duck-billed platypus and the echidna
Chorus

MONOTREMES and MARSUPIALS

Monotremes and marsupials are two distinct orders unique from all others by the way they reproduce: monotremes lay eggs and marsupials develop in pouches. Most live in Australia, Tasmania, New Guinea and the surrounding islands. Only a few species live in South America and only one lives in the United States.

Monotremes and marsupials are not classified according to their jaws, the kind of food they eat or other features mentioned in the last chapter. Unlike the 19 orders of placental mammals, marsupials and monotremes are classified only by how they reproduce. This order classification based only on reproduction fills the marsupial order with a mixture of carnivores (Tasmanian devil, or wolf), herbivores (kangaroo, wombat), and omnivores (opossum, cuscus). To help further clarify their study, scientists sometimes separate the order into suborders that take into account their other features.

MARSUPIALS

Marsupials are the order in which the females have an abdominal pouch called a **marsupium**; Latin for "pouch" or "bag." After a short **gestation** period (developing time in the womb before birth), a tiny, bean-sized baby is born and must crawl to the pouch to survive. Here it will grow and develop, nourished by milk from the mother's mammary glands inside the pouch. The pouch continues to provide a safe place of nourishment and protection until the young are developed.

Kingdom : Animal
Phylum: Vertebrata
Class: Mammal
Order: Marsupialia
Family: Macropodidae
Genus: *Dendrolagus*
Species: *ursinus*

Scientific name:
  Dendrolagus ursinus
Common name:
  Dusky tree kangaroo

Many marsupial families are well known, such as kangaroos and koalas. Less familiar are marsupial wolves, cats and mice; these are similar to their placental mammal counterparts.

KANGAROO

The scientific name for the kangaroo family is derived from a Latin word, *Macropodidae*, meaning "big-footed ones." The 50 species of kangaroos come in a range of sizes from the small 10 inch musky rat kangaroos to the large 8 foot tall greats. The major families include: great, tree, and rat kangaroos, and the wallabies—the medium and small kangaroos.

The young kangaroos are called "joeys." At birth they are blind, furless, and only 3/4 inch long—the size of a beetle! They crawl to the pouch where they will be nourished for several months.

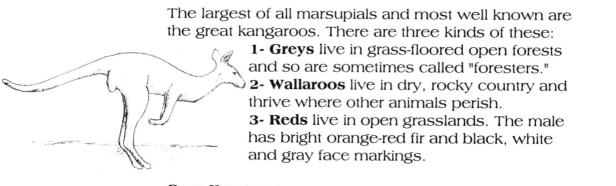

The largest of all marsupials and most well known are the great kangaroos. There are three kinds of these:

1- Greys live in grass-floored open forests and so are sometimes called "foresters."

2- Wallaroos live in dry, rocky country and thrive where other animals perish.

3- Reds live in open grasslands. The male has bright orange-red fir and black, white and gray face markings.

Kangaroos have been known to make giant leaps of 25 to 40 feet in a single bound. Their bodies lean forward with their tails trailing out behind them for balance.

Grey Kangaroo

The greys are the largest marsupials. Males keep growing all their lives and can attain heights of 8 feet and weights of 180 pounds!—These old males are affectionately called "boomers." The average male though, weighs usually about 90 pounds and stands about 6 feet tall. The average female weighs only 50 pounds and reaches 4 feet tall.

The kangaroo's powerful tail helps to balance and support its body when reared upright or when hopping at fast speeds. The tail acts as a "fifth leg" during slow hopping and when the kangaroo is grazing on all fours.

Grey kangaroos are **grazing herbivores**. This means they eat pasture plants such as grasses and herbs but not leaves, bark or fruits of trees. They live where other animals can barely subsist because they are **non-selective eaters**. This means they do not have a preference for particular plants, but eat what is available. These plants usually have poor nutritional value; if greys feed on high quality plants such as oats, their condition actually deteriorates!

Types of herbivores:
1-**browsers** feed on twigs and leaves.
2-**grazers** feed on low plants such as grass

browser

Kangaroos do not perspire or pant to cool themselves as do many other mammals. Instead they lick their forearms, which cools them as the saliva evaporates.

Grey kangaroos live in "mobs" usually comprised of 6 to 12 members. They do not band together when threatened, as do sheep and antelopes. When frightened, they simply scatter in every direction. The males stand upright, make several thumps with their tails before fleeing. The smaller, swifter females make their escape by immediately hopping away.

grazer

KOALA

The scientific name for koala in Latin means "furry, pouched gray bear." It is not really a bear at all, but comprises its own family of marsupials that includes three species:

1- Victoria, the largest, with dark shaggy fur.
2- New South Wales, a mid-sized koala with shaggy fur on its ears
3- Queensland, the smallest.

The **nocturnal** (active at night) koala eats eucalyptus leaves and is the only forest animal to do so. Though it is small in size (about 2 feet long) it can eat over 2 1/2 pounds of leaves, buds, stems and bark in a day!

The koala is arboreal and lives in trees of dense forests. It travels on ground only when necessary to find another tree. Its name in Aborigine means "no drink" because the koala rarely drinks water. It gets moisture through the leaves it eats. The koala even has cheek pouches to carry the leaves until it is ready to eat them at another time.

The front feet have two paws that work like thumbs to help the koala grip branches to climb trees.

For about six months, the young koala is carried in a pouch that opens towards its mother's tail. After emerging, it rides on her back for a few more months by hanging on with strong, long claws.

WOMBAT

The heavily built, bear-looking wombat lives in the forests and grasslands of Australia, Tasmania and nearby islands. It also looks like a husky rat but is usually 3 feet in length and can weigh up to 80 pounds! Wombats usually move slowly, swinging side-to-side in a bear-like gait, but they can also run fast, up to 25 miles per hour!

Wombats, like koalas have pouches that open towards the mother's tail.

Wombats have rodent-like teeth which are ever-growing and must be worn down to keep them from getting too long. They eat roots, grasses, bark and even fungi. Wombats are powerful diggers with spade-shaped paws that are able to dig burrows up to 90 feet long!

The following two wombat species both have acute senses of smell and hearing.
1- Bare-nosed is large and has a soft leathery nose and coarse hair.
2- Hairy-nosed or **soft-furred** has a white furry nose.

OPOSSUMS

The American, or Virginia opossum is the only marsupial that lives in the United States. There are other species of opossum but all are considered rather short on brains. Its braincase, the part of the skull that holds the brain, is one of the smallest of all mammals in proportion to its body.

An amusing experiment graphically shows just how unintelligent the opossum really is. A naturalist measured braincases of similar-weight animals by filling them with dried beans. The higher the intelligence, the more beans the braincase would hold. Here are the results:

> raccoon: 150 beans
> cat: 125 beans
> opossum: 25 beans![1]

In spite of their lack of intelligence, opossums are successful animals for two main reasons—their adaptability to their surroundings and their ability to rapidly reproduce. First opossums are well known for scavenging eggs, small animals and garbage in the neighborhood for their omnivorous diet. In addition, opossums multiply quickly—a female may have a total of 20 babies per year!

Newborn opossums, in spite of being blind and unformed, have well-developed front legs and sharp claws. These enable the young to climb to the pouch immediately after birth, but the claws fall off after the opossum reaches the pouch.

Another special feature that helps the opossum survive is its ability to play dead, or "play possum." When threatened, its heart rate and breathing slow down, its eyes and mouth remain half open and its tongue may hang out—giving the effect of literally "biting the dust." It can keep this posture from a few seconds up to six hours! Even when poked it will not move because even its responsiveness to touch is lessened.

Opossums may also "grin." It is really a warning to others by showing their 50 teeth. That is more teeth than any other animal in America!

The common large Virginia opossum is about as big as a cat. It lives alone in tree stumps or holes in the ground, except during the mating season and while caring for the young. In spite of its lack of intelligence and its tendency to be in the road at the wrong time, it is a very successful mammal.

Some species of opossums have prehensile tails. The tail can act as a another hand, wrapping itself around tree limbs to support the rest of the body.

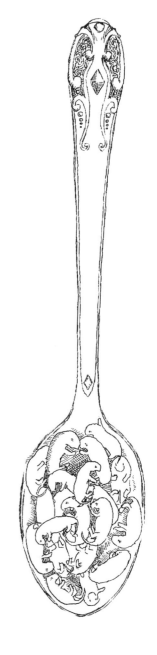

There are about 20 opossum young per teaspoon.

Monotreme eggs are about this size—only 1/2" to 3/4" long!

MONOTREMES

Monotremes are the only mammals that lay eggs. The order includes the duck-billed platypus and the echidna, or spiny anteater. All species in this order live only in Australia, Tasmania and New Guinea.

Scientists have had a difficult time classifying these unique animals. They share characteristics with several kinds of animals such as reptiles and birds. Listed below are some shared features of reptiles and monotremes.

1- They lay shell-covered eggs.
2- They have similar eye structures.
3- They have particularly unique bones in the skull.
4- They have similarities in their digestive, reproductive and excretory systems.

Monotremes are like reptiles.

They are like birds because:
1- They both lay eggs.
2- They both have similar looking skull structures.

Monotremes though, are best described and classified as mammals because they share most mammal characteristics:

1- They both have fur.
2- They both nurse their young with milk.
3- They both are warmblooded (reptiles are coldblooded).

Monotremes are like birds.

Monotremes are considered most similar to marsupials because they have bone structures to support a pouch, whether they have it or not! They are indeed very difficult to classify and so are given their own order which consists of only two families, the platypus and echidna.

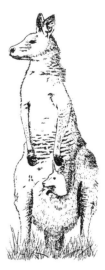

Monotremes are like marsupials.

DUCK-BILLED PLATYPUS

The little duck-billed platypus is only 18 to 20 inches long. In appearance, it seems to be a combination of several kinds of animals because it has a beaver-like tail, duck-like bill and feet and otter-like fur. Males also have an added feature for safety— poison spurs on their ankles with venom strong enough to kill a dog!

Webs on the feet open when the platypus is in the water to help it swim.

The platypus digs well with its sharp-clawed, webbed feet. It makes two types of burrows; only one is shared by the male and female during breeding season. The other is a long burrow (sometimes up to 50 feet long) dug by the female for the eggs and young. The platypus emerges from the water very wet, but apparently the sides of the burrow actually squeeze the water off—the soil absorbs the moisture. The platypus is dry after going into its burrow.

Webs on the front feet are closed and out of the way when the platypus is on land.

The platypus has keen sight and hearing, but when it is in the water its eyes and ears are covered by skin folds. It then relies on its sense of touch through its sensitive skin-covered leathery bill that has many nerve endings. It searches mud and gravel on the bottom of lakes and rivers where it lives to find crayfish, snails, tadpoles, worms and small fish.

The platypus even has cheek pouches to carry its food to the surface. It then eats its food with grinding pads instead of teeth. These strange pads must work well because the platypus has been known to eat half its weight in food a day!

The platypus does not have a pouch, but the mother actually curls herself around the tiny one-inch eggs during incubation. When they hatch, the young are blind and furless. The mother continues to cuddle herself around them to nurse them and keep them warm. At an age of about 4 months the young are fully furred and can survive outside the burrow.

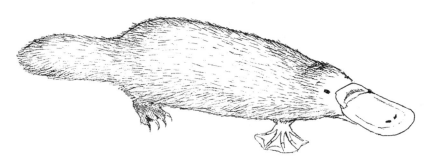

ECHIDNA or SPINY ANTEATER

The echidna is also called the spiny anteater because it has similar characteristics to the true anteater. They each have long snouts, long sticky tongues and similar diets, mainly insects. The echidna is classified as a monotreme because it shares several characteristics with the platypus.

Like the platypus, the echidna lays eggs, but its eggs are very different. They are actually carried in the pouch that exists only during the breeding season. The young are the size of a raisin and break out of their leathery shell with the help of an egg tooth!

Echidnas are covered with fur mixed with barbless spines which, like those of the hedgehog and porcupine, are used for protection. When threatened, the echidna may roll into a ball or quickly dig a hole in record time with its powerful claws. These amazing diggers live under roots, rocks and burrows.

There are two species of echidna.

1- Short-nosed echidnas have a diet consisting of ants and termites. As the name implies, they have short snouts in comparison to the other species. Short-nosed echidnas live in Australia.

2- Long-nosed echidnas have a diet of mainly earthworms and they are the larger species, weighing up to 22 pounds. Some may have a snout that forms two-thirds the length of the head! Long-nosed echidnas have fewer and shorter spines. This species live in New Guinea.

Long-nosed echidna

CARNIVORES and PINNIPEDS

(to the tune of "She'll be Coming Round the Mountain")

This popular folk song was derived from an old spiritual: "When the Chariot Comes." Mountain men took this melody and created "She'll Be Coming Round the Mountain" which became popular with the railroad work crews of the late 1800s.

Unknown

Lyrics by
Dorry and Doug Eldon

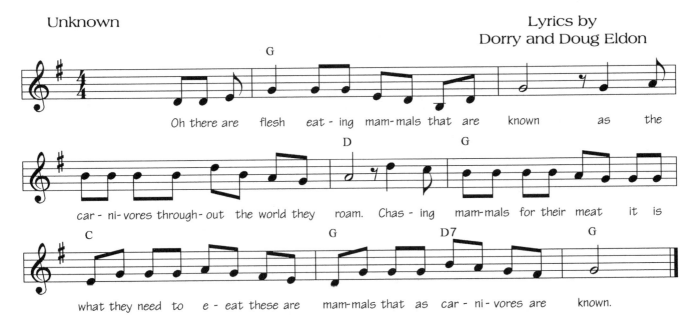

Oh there are flesh eat-ing mam-mals that are known as the car-ni-vores through-out the world they roam. Chas-ing mam-mals for their meat it is what they need to e - eat these are mam-mals that as car - ni-vores are known.

They can smell their food with noses that are long
And their legs are rather muscular and strong
They have claws upon their feet
Helps them hold on to their meat
And their lower jaw is hinged to move so free

Oh the carnivores have specialized back teeth
Carnassials they use for shearing meat
The four canine teeth are pairing
Pointed teeth they use for tearing
Their premolars are for cutting what they eat

In the order there are seven families
Weasels, mongoose and raccoon are three of these
Foxes, wolves, and dogs are canines
All the cats are known as felines
And the others are the bears and the hy—e—nas

Pinnipeds are the aquatic carnivores
And they live out in the ocean or near shores
Sea lion, walrus and seal
How they like fish for their meal
For they are flesh-eating water carnivores

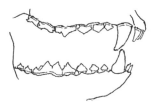

Carnivore—Wolf jaw

Pinniped—Sea lion jaw

CARNIVORES AND PINNIPEDS

The orders of carnivores and pinnipeds are both meat-eaters with similar jaw and teeth configuration. Their similarities end there because carnivores are terrestrial, with features especially suited for catching their prey on land. Pinnipeds are aquatic (marine) and have flippers instead of legs for an oceangoing life.

CARNIVORE CHARACTERISTICS

The Latin for carnivore means "flesh-eater." Basically, carnivores are hunters and everything about them is designed for catching and eating meat. They have long, powerful legs to run and catch their prey; strong, muscular bodies to attack their prey; and teeth especially suited to hold and eat their prey.

The jaws of carnivores are powerful and the lower jaw is attached in such a way that it can move freely in an open/shut, snapping motion. Of course, that is how people move their jaws too. (For manners' sake we learn to eat with our mouths shut, but carnivores cannot—just watch your dog!) This snapping action is different from many other mammals, who may gnaw, in a front-to-back motion; or grind in a side-to-side motion. Carnivores tear and cut their meat, then swallow the pieces whole.

Local domestic carnivores are quite content to eat food other than meat, such as pies, peanut butter sandwiches, cookies and pizza. They particularly enjoy scientific experiments that test their eating habits.

As mentioned earlier, carnivores have specialized teeth for their type of food. They have incisors as do other mammals but their **canine teeth** are especially large—to catch, pierce and hold the prey. Their cheek teeth, the **molars** and **premolars** cut the meat, and the special **carnassials** (near the middle of each side of the jaw) shear the meat.

Carnivores all have four or five claws on each leg for catching and holding their prey. Some carnivores such as cats walk deliCATely and quietly on their toes; others such as bears and raccoons walk cumbersomely along on the soles of their feet.

Kingdom : Animal
Phylum: Vertebrata
Class: Mammal
Order: Carnivora
Family: Felindae
Genus: *Panthera*
Species: leo

Scientific name:
  Panthera leo
Common name:
  Lion

FAMILIES

There are over 238 species of carnivores, but all of these are classified into the following seven families.

1-Dogs   5-Mongooses and relatives
2-Bears   6-Hyenas
3-Raccoons and relatives   7-Cats
4-Weasels and relatives

DOGS, WOLVES, COYOTES, JACKALS, FOXES

The family is called **canid**, **canidae** or **canines**, (the spelling changes depend upon the usage) which refers to the species' long canine teeth. All have characteristic long legs, deep chest, long muzzle, large ears and a bushy tail. They have a keen sense of smell and can smell about 100 times better than people. They need these features, along with good eyesight and hearing, because they have to really work for their food. It just does not grow on trees for them!

These excellent hunters may live in burrows, caves, dens, or even trees. Some members, such as the wolves, live and hunt together in highly developed social packs, while others live solitary lives.

Wolves can be twice as large as coyotes. Wolves run with their tail raised over or held straight out from their body.

Coyotes have larger ears in proportion to their heads than wolves. Coyotes run with their tail down below their body.

BEARS

Bears are large, heavy animals with a characteristic lumbering walk. Yet the polar bear is also a graceful swimmer and especially suited for aquatic life. Bears have large heads, small ears and small eyes; their sense of smell, however, is good, as with other carnivores. A few of the more familiar species are the black, grizzly, polar, and spectacled bear of South America. The Kodiak bear of Alaska is the largest carnivore; it weighs over 1,650 pounds!

The family of bears, called **ursid**, are omnivores (except the carnivorous polar bear) that eat a variety of meat and plant material. Their premolar and molar, or cheek, teeth are blunted for grinding leaves, fruit and other plant materials.

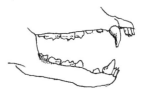

Bears have blunted cheek teeth for grinding plant material.

The grizzly bear may hibernate, or sleep during the winter months, while it lives off the stored fat in its body.

RACCOONS

The raccoon has long been a favorite in American folklore with its crafty, curious, intelligent nature. The family though, also includes the long-nosed coatimundi of the Southwestern United States, the ringtail and even several species of pandas!

Raccoons have a bear-like walk; they use the soles of their feet with their heels touching the ground. They are also good tree climbers and several species live in trees while others live in crevices among rocks.

Raccoons like to handle things, especially food, with their sensitive hands. They like to wash them after eating.

WEASELS, BADGERS, SKUNKS, OTTERS, WOLVERINES

This family, **mustelids**, (for *must*, which means odor or scent) are skillful hunters, who have often been hunted themselves for their thick, luscious fur. They all have scent glands for protection or identification, and they usually have long, slender bodies. They have short ears and many have **non-retractile** claws—claws that are always stretched out ready to pierce. Species in this family live in trees, burrows, crevices, or even in the ocean. There are 23 genera and 64 species, only a few of which are mentioned here.

Badger

Sea otters played a large part in the history of Northern California where Russian ships hunted them for their thick, warm fur.

Weasels are long and slender with short legs and tails. Considered fierce fighters, they include minks, ferrets, and polecats.

Badgers are extremely good diggers that have short, stocky bodies weighing up to 37 pounds.

Skunks have black and white fur of various patterns that warns animals to stay away or get sprayed by a bitter scent.

Otters include both the freshwater river otter and the sea otter. They have webbing between their toes to help them swim.

Wolverines are powerful and fierce enough to drive even bears away from their food.

It is best to go the other way when you cross a skunk's path!

MONGOOSES, CIVETS

There are over 30 genera and 70 species of mongoose and their relatives. Members of this family have short legs, long bushy tails, long heads and pointed muzzles and a cat-like walk. They usually live alone, but may live in groups or bands. The mongoose is an omnivore but has been used to hunt poisonous snakes.

The mongoose dodges a snake's repeated strikes until the snake grows tired. The mongoose then feeds on a tasty meal.

HYENAS, AARDWOLVES

Members of this family have front legs that are longer than the back legs, giving them a strange sloping appearance. They live in Africa and parts of Asia in caves, brush or abandoned burrows.

Hyenas may live together in large groups called **clans**. They may feed on **carrion** (dead animals) or hunt, either alone or with others. They make their laughing sound after a kill. Hyenas' powerful jaws are able to crush bones.

Aardwolves have jaws that are so weak they cannot eat meat! Instead they eat termites and insect larvae!

Hyena

Aardwolf

The cheetah is the fastest land mammal and can run up to 70 m.p.h. for short distances.

CATS

The members of the family of **felines** have strong muscular bodies covered with soft, thick fur. These hunters have acute senses of smell, hearing and sight. Cats have long, curved, sharp claws that **retract** when not in use. Cats walk on their toes rather than on the soles of their feet, enabling them to stalk their prey quietly.

Many cats live alone, although several of the large cats, such as the lions, live in social structures with well-defined roles.

Cats thrive in a variety of habitats. They are able to climb, leap and swim well; there is even a cat that lives entirely on its fishing ability. Listed are the four different genera of cats.

1- Small cats are the cats that cannot roar. As their name implies, they are usually small in size when compared to other wild species. They include cougars, lynxes and domestic cats.

2- Large cats are those that can roar. They include the lion, jaguar, tiger, and leopard.

3- Cheetahs cannot fully retract their claws, as can all other cats. Their teeth and small dome-like skulls are also unique, as is their hunting technique—they do not stalk or sneak up on their prey but run after it.

4- Clouded leopards have unusual fur markings of dark ovals and circles resembling clouds. They have spots on their heads, legs and at the base of their tail, with stripes on the remainder of their tail. They have an unusual teeth configuration, featuring upper canines longer than any other cat's.

Fur patterns

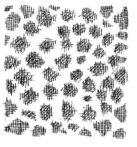

Cheetah

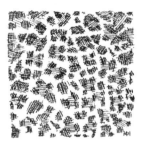

Leopard

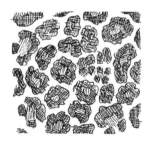

Jaguar

The domestic cat is descended from wild small cats.

The tiger is the largest of all cats.

PINNIPEDS

The order's name means "feather-footed ones" because the species all have webbed front and back flippers. These marine mammals eat fish and sea life from the cold waters where they live. As previously mentioned, pinnipeds' teeth are similar to those in the order of carnivores. They have large canine teeth for catching and grasping, and cheek teeth for chewing up their food.

There are three families of pinnipeds each with distinctive distinguishing features.
> **1- Walruses** whose tusks are actually enlarged canine teeth.
> **2- True seals** with fat roly-poly bodies, awkward on land, graceful in water.
> **3- Sea Lions and Fur or Eared Seals** with powerful flippers that help them move on land.

WALRUS
The Latin name for walrus means "one who walks with its teeth." Walruses can use their tusks, which can be up to 3 feet long, to drag their heavy bodies along on land. Walruses also have thick mustaches that may contain 700 coarse whiskers to feel for food while swimming in dark or murky waters.

Walruses have blubber instead of fur to insulate them from the cold Arctic waters where they live. As much as half a walrus' body weight is blubber—up to 4 inches thick! Walruses live in herds and gather on ice packs to breed and bundle together for warmth. The walrus can tuck its hind flippers under its body, helping it to move about on land or ice.

The walrus usually weighs 2,000 pounds but can weigh up to 3,500 pounds and grow to 13 feet long! Even with its massive body it is only the second largest pinniped—the largest is the elephant seal.

Walrus jaw

Kingdom :	Animal
Phylum:	Vertebrata
Class:	Mammal
Order:	Carnivora
Family:	Odobenidae
Genus:	*Odobenus*
Species:	*rosmarus*

Scientific name:
  Odobenus rosmarus
Common name:
  Walrus

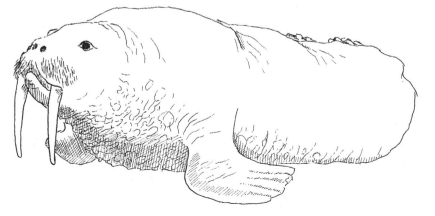

SEALS (TRUE, EARLESS, OR HAIR SEALS)
The seal is awkward on land because it cannot tuck its flippers under its body to help it move. Though clumsy on land, it is very graceful in its natural element, water. With a torpedo-shaped body, it cuts the water and maneuvers easily. The seal propels itself with its hind flippers and steers with its front flippers.

Seals do not have ear flaps.

The seal family usually includes small species such as the harp seal and the Hawaiian monk seal. But the largest of all pinnipeds, the elephant seal, is a true seal. The elephant seal gets its name from the male's huge nose which droops like an elephant's trunk. It can even be inflated during mating season as a show of might and strength. A male elephant seal may be 20 feet long and weigh 3 tons!

In many mammal species, the male is much larger than the female; this is called **sexual dimorphism**. The elephant seal clearly shows this characteristic: the male is three times larger than the female!

To mate, give birth and feed their young, many species of pinnipeds **haul out**, which means they gather in large numbers on shores after migrating to them from many miles.

Crabeater seals eat krill, (small crustaceans), not crab. The unusual teeth strain the krill from the water in the seal's mouth.

SEA LIONS, FUR or EARED SEALS
At first glance it is difficult to tell if a graceful swimming pinniped is a true seal, or a sea lion. There are several differences between the two families, but the easiest to recognize is the presence of ear flaps in sea lions and eared seals.

Sea lions are usually the larger of the two families, and are so named because many have a short lion-like mane. Unlike seals, sea lions use their front flippers to swim and their rear flippers to steer through the water. They are not as helpless as seals on land because they can use their back flippers to walk by tucking them up under their bodies.

Species include the California Sea Lion, and the Alas-kan or Northern Fur seals. Like other pinnipeds, sea lions haul out in large masses. For example, 1.5 million Alaskan Fur seals haul out at Pribilof Island in the Bering Sea.

SEAL AND SEA LION DIFFERENCES

Species of the seal and sea lion families may look similar, but major distinguishing characteristics are listed below:

True, or Earless Seals	Sea Lions, or Eared Seals
1- no ear flaps	1- noticeable external ears
2- cannot tuck its hind flippers under its body	2- can tuck its hind flippers under its body
3- short front flippers are used for steering	3- long front flippers are main power for swimming
4- hind flippers are main power for swimming	4- hind flippers are used for steering

The sea lion is able to do special tricks—except it can do them just right to draw a crowd.

California Sea Lion

UNGULATES
HOOFED MAMMALS
(to the tune of "Home on the Range")

The theory is that "Home on the Range" started as a poem by Dr. Brewster Higley
in the 1870s. It is thought his neighbor, Dan Kelley added the tune. The song
became very popular 1930s as it was played over a new invention—the radio.

Dan Kelley   Lyrics by Doug Eldon

The ungulates can, be important to man
After years of domestication
They help to provide, clothes from their fur and hide
Meat, milk, and transportation

CHORUS #2 Oh, at home on the range
The grasslands where the hoofed mammals graze
They're cursorial, which means that they run well
To escape being carnivores' prey

The zebra and horse and the donkey of course
One-toed animals no one forgets
The kinds with three toes, the tapirs and rhinos
Are the odd-numbered toed ungulates
CHORUS #1

The order that's left, all have hoofs that are cleft
Two or four toes and there's many kinds
Sheep, cattle and goat, pronghorn, elk, antelope
Giraffe, camel, deer, hippo, and swine

The difference between horns and antlers is seen
Every year when the antlers are shed
For horns do not fall but are part of the skull
And remain on the animal's head
CHORUS #2

UNGULATES
HOOFED MAMMALS

Ungulates, or hoofed mammals, eat plant material and so are classified as herbivores. (The only exceptions are the omnivorous pigs and peccaries.) The families are placed in two orders which are determined by their number of toes.

1- Odd-toed: equines, tapirs and rhinoceroses.
2- Even-toed: pigs, peccaries, hippos, camels, chevrotains, deer, giraffes, pronghorns and bovines (the cattle and antelope species).

Ungulates are no match for carnivores' claws and jaws; instead, they use their long, strong legs to escape. Ungulates are **cursorial** mammals, which means they can run very, very fast. They run on the tips of their toes which have hardened hoofs (actually toenails) that help protect their feet.

For additional protection, many ungulates live in herds and have a herding instinct that keeps them together when threatened. Though their best defense is usually to run, the musk oxen will form a circle around their young when attacked by carnivores.

The cursorial ability of ungulates has made them extremely useful for transportation. Horses have carried men into battle and camels have walked caravans over the desert for centuries. Many other species have been domesticated (made tame) to provide wool, skins, milk and meat.

The horse is an
odd-toed ungulate.

Kingdom :   Animal
Phylum: Vertebrata
Class: Mammal
Order: Perissodactyla
Family: Equidae
Genus: *Equus*
Species: *caballus*

Scientific name:
  Equus caballus
Common name:
  Horse

The goat is an
even-toed ungulate.

ODD-TOED
If the odd-toed ungulate's feet were compared to human's, a hoof would be considered the middle toe. This is the toe that bears the weight of the animal. The three families of the odd-toed ungulates include:

1- Equines—horses, donkeys (asses), zebras
2- Tapirs
3- Rhinoceroses

HORSES, DONKEYS and ZEBRAS
The **equine** family includes the horses, donkeys and zebras. Domesticated horses and donkeys have played large parts in human history as they carried people and their burdens to new areas.

A horse hoof has
only one visible toe.

A rhino's hoof has
three toes. The middle
toe bears the weight
of the animal.

HORSE

The 200 breeds of domestic horses are all descendents of two kinds of wild horses. The southern species lived in the hot deserts of North Africa and Asia and are now extinct. Their descendents are the swift Arabian-type breeds.

The northern species are from the cold areas of Europe and Asia. Only one species of wild horse remains, the endangered Przewalski, that lives in the Gobi Desert of Mongolia. Descendents of the northern wild horse are the strong, stocky, heavy-boned horses and ponies, such as the Exmoor ponies of England.

Horses have strong muscular bodies and unlike donkeys or zebras, have long manes. Their cheek teeth are made for grinding plants—they bite plants off with their incisors and chew them up with their molars.

For centuries horses have been domesticated for work and pleasure.

The domestic horse comes in a variety of sizes and builds, from the stout workhorses, to the petite miniature horses—the pets of past queens.

Horse Talk
Foal: up to 1 year old
Colt: male up to 3 years
Filly: female up to 3 years
Stallion: male more than 3 years
Mare: female more than 3 years old
Gelding: male horse that has been neutered

Mustang: domestic horse that lives in the wild
Mule: part donkey and horse

DONKEY or ASS

The domesticated donkey is thought to have come from the Nubian wild ass of Africa. Although now extinct, its striped-leg descendents still live near the Nile. The donkey, ass or burro (Spanish for donkey), has a stocky body, a short mane that stands up, and a tail with only long tufts of hair at the end.

The donkey is considered the "poor man's horse" and is still the main beast of burden and means of transportation in many parts of the world. In early Western American history a prospector would be a fool to hunt for gold without his sure-footed "desert canary"—so named for its loud bray.

In religious literature, donkeys are noted as being valuable partners of important events. The Bible records an ass speaking to a foolish prophet, and Hindu writings mention donkeys pulling a chariot of cosmic gods. Buddhists write of a donkey's witnessing the birth of Buddha, and the Moslem Koran mentions a strange beast speaking with the voice of a donkey. In addition, it is said that the domestic donkey's cross on its back (down the center and across the shoulders) came as a reward for carrying Jesus.

"Desert canary"

In spite of the impressive roles they have played, donkeys are often shunned and scorned as fools. *Pinocchio* tells of rebellious, disobedient boys turning into donkeys and a foolish person, in one of Shakespeare's plays, is reminded to "not make an ass of himself." Unfortunately, there are reasons for these characterizations because donkeys are known for their stubborn, strong will—ask anyone who has one!

This donkey is loaded with food for local tortoises. Today, the donkey is still the main beast of burden.

ZEBRA

Without its stripes, the African zebra would look very similar to the donkey. The zebra has a donkey's characteristic stocky body, short mane that stands up, and a tail with only a tuft of hair at the end. The ancient Roman name for zebra means "tiger horse," but the zebra has never been tamed like the horse or donkey.

The three species of zebras live in Africa and are distinguished by their pattern of stripes, where they live and their ear and body size.

> **1- Plains Zebras** are pony-size and may graze in herds but live together in family groups.
> **2- Mountain Zebras** are pony-size and may also graze in herds but live in family groups.
> **3- Grevy's Zebras** are the largest and have large hairy ears. They sometimes live in family groups but may often live alone.

Zebras have unique stripes, no two zebras look exactly alike.

TAPIR

This ungulate looks part elephant with its short trunk-like nose, and part swine with its round, plump body that tapers in the front. The tapir is about the size of a donkey but has a low, narrow mane and short, thick tail. It is a very agile climber and runner with its short, slender legs.

Tapirs live near water in humid tropical forests of Mexico, Central and South America and Southeastern Asia. They are good swimmers and delight to splash and play in the water.

Tapir

The tapir has keen senses of hearing and smell and burrows in search of young plant shoots—a favorite food.

Rhino

RHINOCEROS

The name, Rhinoceros, is a very descriptive one because it means "horned nose." The characteristic horn is made of solidified hair-like fiber which grows from the skin. The African rhino's front horn grows from 18 to 48 inches— the longest ever recorded was 65 inches!

Rhinos have massive bodies and are the second largest land mammals—along with the hippos. Some males are over six feet tall at the shoulders and weigh over three tons!

Rhinos live in a variety of habitats: in hills and mountains, open grasslands, swamps, or even deep, dense forests. The species can be divided into two groups, classified by their horns.

1- One-horned rhinos include the Indian with two small tusks, and the Javan.

2- Two-horned rhinos include the Sumatran or "hairy" rhino and two African species: the black, and the square-lipped, also called white (a mispronunciation of the Dutch "wide"— referring to its lips).

Egrets, oxpeckers, mynas eat ticks and flies off the rhino's back.

The strong, thick-skinned rhino— its horn in particular, has long been considered to hold many curative powers. During the Middle Ages kings drank from rhino horn goblets to detect poison. A corrosive poison would react with the horn and give the liquid a milk-like appearance. The rhino's possible medicinal qualities account for its value to poachers ready to sell the horn and other body parts on the black market.

EVEN-TOED UNGULATES

Odd- and even-toed mammals share similar characteristics: they are both cursorial and herbivorous, but are classified into separate orders determined by their number of toes. The scientific name for the order of even-toed ungulates is artiodactyls. The word *artio* means "even," *dactyl* means "toe" or "finger."

The most common kind of ungulates are two-toed; often called "cloven-hoofed" or "split-hoofed." Many species live in herds for protection and several have unique stomachs to help digestion of plant material.

Deer
The hoofs are on each tip of the third and fourth toes— the other toes are either very small or absent.

Camel
The camel has pads on its feet that spread out so it can easily walk on sand.

The nine families of even-toed ungulates are loosely divided into the following three groups.

1- Pigs, peccaries, and **hippos** have barrel-shaped bodies and may include species with an omnivorous diet (exceptions in this otherwise herbivorous order).

2- Camels and relatives are herbivores that eat plants low in nutrients. The food is swallowed and later brought up for chewing before being digested. They are **cud chewers,** with three-part or chambered stomachs.

3- True ruminants or **cud chewers** are the even-toed ungulates with four-chambered stomachs. They can ingest large amounts of plant material that can be swallowed quickly with little chewing. The food later comes back up in the form of **cud** to be chewed more thoroughly at another time.

The ability to chew the cud actually lets these mammals "eat and run" so they can digest their food in a safer place. The two major groups of true ruminants include:

1- deer, giraffe, pronghorn

2- **bovine**; hollow-horned ruminants consisting of several subfamilies

Even-toed families:
Pig
Peccary
Hippo
Camel
Mouse Deer
Deer
Giraffe
Pronghorn
Bovine

PIGS AND PECCARIES

The **suid** family includes both domestic and wild pigs. Peccaries are similar but look like smaller, more delicate pigs. Both families have four toes, but only the middle two are hoofed—the outer two do not even reach the ground.

Pigs are omnivores and eat anything from fungi and grass to small animals and birds. Some species, such as the warthog, have ridges on their faces which are skin growths without any bone supporting them. Their upper and lower canine teeth may grow outward or upward to form dangerous, powerful tusks.

The peccaries are a separate family, though they do have the hog-like body. They have more bristly hair than hogs, but their legs are long and skinny and their hooves are very small. If the peccaries have tusks, they are pointed down, instead of up and outward like pigs'.

Warthog

HIPPOPOTAMUS

The two kinds of hippo are very different in size, but they both share the hippo charact-eristics: a barrel-shaped body, a huge mouth, a wide snout and short, heavy legs. They have four toes and have a three-part, chambered stomach that helps digest the grasses they eat.

The hippo has protruding eyes that help it see out of the water without lifting its whole head.

The incisor and canine teeth grow continuously and the lower canine teeth look rather tusk-like. Hippos are amphibious animals, being equally comfortable in land or water. They live among the reeds and grasslands of the Nile Valley with water always nearby.

The hippo, along with the rhino, is considered the second largest land mammal, weighing up to 10,000 pounds!

The pygmy hippo looks like a miniature hippo and only weighs up to 600 pounds. Other features distinguish it: the head is a different shape with eyes that do not protrude as do the larger hippo's. The pygmy hippo is hairless except for a few bristles around its mouth, and it has only two lower incisors.

CAMEL

The **camelid** family includes **camels, llamas, alpacas, guanaco, vicuna**. Camels are the only species that live in Africa and Asia; they are much larger than their llama relatives that live in the high altitudes of western South America.

The hippo has special pores that secrete "blood sweat;" an oily protective substance that allows the hippo to stay in the water or stay in a very dry atmosphere for long periods of time.

All camels have small heads, long, thin necks and divided (**cleft**) upper lips. These ungulates have three-part stomachs instead of four-part and so are not true ruminants (see next section). All species have two toes with a large pad between them. The pad stretches out wide to help the animals walk through sand without sinking.

Dromedary camel

Camels include the one-hump **dromedary** (also called **Arabian**) of the North African and Asian deserts, and the furry two-hump **Bactrian** of the high, rocky desert mountains of Asia.

Camels are the only animals that can live in the hot dry desert and carry large loads. They can outlast other animals in the desert because they can go without water for long periods of time.

The camel's hump is full of fat and can weigh up to 80 pounds! It lives off this stored fat when food is not available. A camel can lose up to 40 percent of its body weight and keep on going. Other features protect the camel from the desert sands: closeable nostrils and long eyelashes. There are even inner eyelids to wash away sand if it gets in its eyes.

Llamas, guanacos, alpacas and vicunas do not have humps, but are the South American camels of the high altitude of the Andes Mountains in Peru, Ecuador, and Bolivia.

Bactrian camel
Species in the camel family are grazers.

Guanacos and vicuna are the wild species. Guanacos often live in small herds in dry, open plains or mountains. Vicunas are smaller and have teeth unlike any other species in this family: ever-growing incisors on their lower jaws that must be continually worn down through wear. They were nearly hunted to extinction for their wool, which is the finest of any animal. Today, the native human population harvests the fibers.

Llamas are large, sure-footed and often used as pack animals. The Incas domesticated and used 300,000 of them as beasts of burden in their silver mines before the Spanish conquest.

Alpacas look like smaller long-haired llamas and are often raised for their wool. Garments made from the Alpaca clothed ancient Inca royalty.

RUMINANTS OR CUD CHEWERS
True ruminants have four-part stomachs that help digest plant food. These are the most common even-toed ungulates and often live in herds on prairies and grasslands. Many common barnyard ruminating animals, such as cattle, sheep and goats, were domesticated from wild species long ago.

Stomach diagram
The food is swallowed unchewed or barely chewed, and goes directly to the rumen, where bacteria and protozoa begin digestion. When the animal is resting, or away from its enemies, the food is brought back up, rechewed and swallowed.

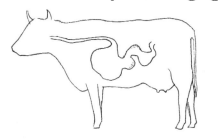

MOUSE DEER or CHEVROTAIN

One of the smallest ungulates, the mouse deer looks part deer and part rodent. It walks in a stiff-legged manner on very thin legs—only the diameter of a pencil in some species! The mouse deer has no upper incisors, but the males have upper tusks that can sometimes be seen just below the upper lip.

DEER

The large family of deer includes 17 genera and 38 species. Among them are the unusual pudu and hog deer and also the well-known elk and moose, the giant of the deer family. They are all long-legged ungulates that often live in herds in various habitats of forests, deserts, tundra, and swamps. Species of the deer family are all ruminants and feed on grasses, twigs, bark and other plant parts.

Males in the deer family are the only mammals that have antlers. They begin growing in the early summer when the deer is one or two years old. Though they are shed in winter after the mating season, they will grow larger and more elaborate each year until they reach adult length and shape. The major characteristics of antlers are:

1- They are shed every year.
2- They are made of bone and covered with a thin skin called **velvet**, that protects the growing antlers and rubs off in the fall.
3- They identify adult male deer species.
4- They may branch.

Elk or wapiti
Each year the antlers add points (like branches) until the characteristic shape of the species is attained. The moose has the heaviest antlers (90 pounds); the elk has the longest (nearly 6 feet)!

GIRAFFE and OKAPI

Giraffes and okapis are classified in the same family though they do not seem to resemble each other. Giraffes are the tallest mammals known, with characteristic long legs, neck and tail. Their horns are very unique. They are present at birth as little knobs with a bony core and grow slowly throughout the giraffe's life. They become fused with the skull and shed velvety hair but not the skin.

The okapis have shorter necks and strong, muscular builds. The males have small, skin-covered horns. Their coloration ranges from deep red to almost black—the legs and hindquarters are black and white striped. They are rare animals that live in the dense, damp forests of Zaire and were only discovered in the early 1900s.

PRONGHORN

North America's pronghorn are often called "pronghorn antelopes," but they are not true antelopes. Antelopes are members of the bovine family (see below) that grow horns, which by definition are never shed. Pronghorns, instead, have horns and shed part of them. They have a permanent bony core over which a hollow horn grows that falls off yearly.

Pronghorns live on the plains of North America. They provided food for early pioneers and are sometimes thought of as America's antelope. Pronghorns can run at high speeds (up to 53 miles per hour) for long distances and depend on this and their keen eyesight for protection from carnivores.

The pronghorn is able to raise its hair by special muscles. When it is cold it keeps its hair flat, but if it is too warm, it will raise the hair to allow the air to cool its skin.

Pronghorns have one-prong horns that may grow up to 20 inches in length.

♪♪♪♪♪♪

"Oh give me a home where the buffalo roam Where the deer and the antelope play...."

The antelope in the pioneer song, "Home on the Range" refers to the pronghorn because there are no antelopes in America.

♪♪♪♪♪♪

ANTELOPE, CATTLE, BISON, BUFFALO, GOAT AND SHEEP

The **bovine** family includes species that range from the stocky buffaloes to the slender gazelles and agile mountain goats. There are over 120 species, including cattle, goats, sheep, and exotic and unusual African and Central Asian antelope species.

Bovines:
1-are herbivorous
2-are ruminants
3-have horns

Bovines eat by twisting grass or other plant material around their tongues and biting off the plant with their lower incisors.

Horns are a major characteristic of this family; most males and many females grow them. Horns are quite different from antlers.

    1- They are made of **keratin**—like claws and fingernails.

    2- They grow out of the head and are not shed; they stay on for life. The age of the animal can be determined by the length of the horns.

    3- Horns can be hollow or have a core of bone.

    4- True horns never branch.

Because there is such wide variety in the bovine family, scientists divide them into several subfamilies, including

> **1-** cattle, bison and relatives
> **2-** antelopes and relatives which include three separate subfamilies
> **3-** goats and sheep

CATTLE

Cattle are a type of oxen and were first domesticated in the region of Iraq where they used oxen to pull their wagons. Drawings from Ancient Egypt illustrate longhorn, shorthorn and polled (those born without horns) cattle. Today there are about 1.2 billion domestic cattle around the world!

Kingdom :	Animal
Phylum:	Vertebrata
Class:	Mammal
Order:	Artiodactyla
Family:	Bovidae
Genus:	*Bison*
Species:	*bison*

Scientific name:
  Bison bison
Common name:
  American bison or
  Buffalo

The two types of domestic cattle are the Indian and European. Though similar, the Indian has a large, fatty lump on its shoulder and dewlaps (folds of skin) under its chin. The Brahma bulls seen in rodeos are Indian; dairy cows such as Holstein, and beef cattle such as Hereford and Angus, are European.

Wild species include, of course, the American buffalo, which is a really a bison. (The term "buffalo" refers to the water buffalo; it does not have a hump on its back.) The bison stands about six feet high and weighs up to 2,200 pounds. It is a huge ungulate that once numbered 50 million in the United States! They fed and clothed the American Indians of the Great Plains for centuries, but by the late 1800s only 600 bison were left. Heroic preservation efforts have been successful in saving the bison from extinction and today there are over 40,000.

ANTELOPES

Antelopes can run or leap quickly with their long legs and strong hindquarters. Each species of antelope has a unique set of horns that does not branch as do deer antlers. Instead, the horns may be curved or straight, and long or short. The 70 species vary considerably from the four pound rabbit-sized dik diks to the 1,900-pound, ox-like elands. Many though, have a slender, graceful body, like the gazelle.

Most antelopes live in savannas, or treed grasslands, of Africa, though some species live in Asia. Antelopes do not live in the United States. Many species, such as the eland, live in herds while others live alone. All are herbivorous, but some are **grazers** (eating only low grasses) while others are **browsers** (eating leaves and twigs).

Many antelopes **migrate** (travel from place to place) for warmth or food as seasons change. They have keen senses of smell and eyesight to watch for their carnivorous enemies' approach. When predators come, antelopes run with all their cursorial might—but many still provide a rich food source for carnivores!

GOATS AND SHEEP

Goats are **caprines** and sheep are **ovines**, large subfamilies of bovines. This group includes both the wild species and their domestic barnyard descendents.

Goat

All wild goats live in Europe and the Himalaya Mountains in Asia—except the American Rocky Mountain goat. Domestic breeds are thought to have descended from wild Persian goats of Asia. The three major kinds of domestic goats include: the Swiss goats with pointed ears, the Nubian with hanging ears, and the woolly goats, such as the Cashmere and Angora.

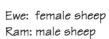

Ewe: female sheep
Ram: male sheep

Three species of wild sheep in North America include: the Rocky Mountain Bighorn, the Dall's sheep, and the Stone's sheep. Many domestic breeds of sheep are thought to have come from a wild Mouflon species taken to the European mainland from a small island off of Italy in the 1800s.

Sheep

General Differences:

Goat	Sheep
1- lean body	1- fat body
2- usually hairy, bearded	2- woolly (wild sheep—hairy)
3- females are often horned	3- females are often hornless
4- horns sweep upward and curve toward back	4- horns grow outward from the side of forehead and may twirl like springs

Goat on sheep!

PRIMATES

(to the tune of "Abraham's Daughters" or "Raw Recruits")

Though little known today, "Abraham's Daughters" was one of the most popular Civil War songs. It was written by a successful songwriter who also penned: "Listen to the Mocking Bird," "Oh Where, Oh Where Has My Little Dog Gone" and "Ten Little Indians."

Septimus Winner   Lyrics by Dorry and Doug Eldon

Oh we pri-mates are the mam-mals that have five fing-ers and five toes, op-

pos-ing thumbs help us to grasp on to the things that we hold. We

have large eyes, they all face front, that help us, just for in-stance to

judge the depth of things close by and things off in the dis-tance, to

judge the depth of things close by and things off in the dis-tance.

There are fourteen families of us in this whole primate order
Lesser and great ape, two marmosets, the loris and the tarsier
Chorus

Three lemurs and the aye aye and the New and Old World monkeys
The human being but don't forget the so unusual Indris.
Chorus

Humans have large heads that hold big brains we use to our advantage
For problem solving, making tools, the oral and the written language
Chorus

PRIMATES

The primates include a wondrous array of mammals ranging from little wide-eyed lorises to us—humans, known scientifically as *homo sapiens*. The human resemblance to other primates can be startling! But then, all 14 primate families share many features unique only to the primate order.

Primates have forward-facing eyes to perceive depth or dimension. Many animals in other orders have eyes on the sides of their heads; ducks, for example, have to turn their head to look at things.

Another unique feature of primates is their relatively large heads. Actually, scientists say that primates have large braincases in proportion to their bodies. This feature makes room for big brains, or high intelligence. Of all primates, humans have the largest braincases for their size. Great apes—the family of chimpanzees, orangutans and gorillas—come in a close second.

Primate arms and legs are usually long, with four or five fingers on hands, and four or five toes on feet. The thumbs and big toes (except human toes) are often **opposable**, which means the hands and feet can easily hold onto things. This makes for great tree-climbing abilities, and indeed, most primates are arboreal.

Like most other mammals, primates have four kinds of teeth: incisors, canines, premolars, and molars. Some primates have very large canines that help them eat meat, but they do not have the other specialized teeth of the carnivores. Other primates have teeth suited for a herbivorous diet of leaves and other plant parts.

LORIS

The family of large, wide-eyed lorises is comprised of 12 species including the lesser-known pottos and galagos. This family lives in Africa, parts of Asia and the Philippines. Their diet consists of fruit, plants, insects and even small animals.

Most species are nocturnal, and like most primates, lorises are arboreal. Lorises and pottos are usually slow movers with hand-over-hand motions; they may move quickly, but do not jump or leap. In contrast, galagos move by jumping.

Primates may have opposable thumbs and toes to help them grasp things such as food, branches and vines.

Many primates have a **prehensile** tail, meaning a tail that can act like another hand to grasp branches.

Kingdom : Animal
Phylum: Vertebrata
Class: Mammal
Order: Primate
Family: Lorisidae
Genus: *Loris*
Species: *tardigradus*

Scientific name:
Loris tardigradus
Common name:
Slender loris

Galago

LEMUR TYPES
Three distinct lemur families live on Madagascar, or other islands off the east coast of Africa. All three families have long snouts and wet noses. They are further classified into families by their behavior and bone structures. Indris, a fourth lemur-like family, share similarities in appearance and habitat.

LEMUR
Lemurs have thick, soft, woolly hair and long, furry tails. Their bodies and limbs are long and thin and most have large eyes like the lorises. They eat plants, insects and small mammals and may use the serrated, comb-like teeth on their lower jaw for scooping out fruit or eating tough bamboo plants.

Lemurs can be quick runners when on the ground, and some species are even semiaquatic.

DWARF LEMUR, MOUSE LEMUR
These lemurs are very agile. The dwarf lemur moves among branches with a squirrel-like scurrying; the mouse lemur either walks on all fours or leaps. The mouse lemur is the smallest primate, growing to only five inches (not measuring the tail).

Both lemurs eat insects, fruit, flowers and sometimes smaller animals such as birds or lizards. They have the unique ability to store fat in their tails to be used by their bodies if food becomes scarce. Because of this trait they may be called "fat-tailed lemurs."

WEASEL, OR SPORTIVE LEMUR
Unlike the other lemurs, this lemur's head is short with large, round, furless ears. The true lemur has short- to medium-length furry ears.

INDRI
Indris consist of three genera and like the lemurs, live only on Madagascar. Indris are large with a short tail and silky fur. The avahis are small with long tails and woolly fur. The sifakas are of medium size with silky, usually white fur, long tails and hairless faces.

The members of this family are **clinger-leapers**—they cling and leap from branch to branch. But they may use hand-over-hand motions when climbing. They have fewer teeth than any other primate and use them for eating leaves, buds, flowers and other plant parts.

The mouse lemur is only 5 inches long and the smallest of all primates.

The ring-tailed lemur is a true lemur.

Sifaka

Indri

AYE AYE

The aye aye also live on Madagascar. They are slender, have a bushy tail and course, straight hair. They have large furless ears and very long fingers with claw-like nails. The third fingers are especially long and used for digging insects from the stems of bamboo or other plants.

Aye ayes have rodent-like front teeth, which means they are ever-growing and constantly need to be worn down. Teeth of this kind are very unusual for monkeys.

TARSIER

The family name refers to the tarsier's long tarsal, or ankle, bone. These primates live in the bushy forest or scrub vegetation of Malaysia. Tarsiers are clinger-leapers. Their movements have been compared to those of frogs because they can make such quick jumps with so little effort!

The tarsier can rotate its head almost 360 degrees! Its eyes are even larger in relation to its head than the lemur's —its eyesight and field of vision is excellent. The tarsier hunts insects and chews them up in a side-to-side motion.

MARMOSET, TAMARIN

Species in this family are small, usually the size of a squirrel. Among them is the pygmy marmoset, which is only six inches in length! The two genera, marmosets and tamarins, can be recognized most easily by comical, delightful hair tufts on their heads Their faces are usually hairless and the rest of their body is covered with very dense, soft fur.

Marmosets and tamarins live in the rainforests of Central and South America. There they live in large groups in trees, feeding on insects and fruit. They have claws instead of fingernails and use them to help each other preen—grooming their soft, pretty fur. Tamarins are different from marmosets in that they have large canine teeth and no ear tufts.

GOELDI'S MARMOSET

This marmoset combines features from the marmoset and New World monkey families. The face, foot and claw-like nails are like the marmoset's. The skull structure and teeth configuration are like the New World monkey's. These marmosets live together in large bands of 20 to 30 members in the rainforests of the upper Amazon.

The aye aye's long ears can hear insects in the bark. Their long, clawed third finger digs them out.

Tarsier

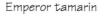

Emperor tamarin

Goeldi's Marmoset

The howler monkey is a New World monkey.

NEW WORLD MONKEYS

"New World" refers to the Americas where these monkeys live. They are usually much larger than marmosets and some have prehensile tails. Their nostrils are far apart and open to the sides rather than to the front, as human nostrils do. They have fingernails instead of claws. Not all have opposable thumbs but their big toe is opposable. The New World monkeys are very agile and swing smoothly through the trees— marmosets and tamarins have jerky movements.

The family includes many species with a typical monkey-like appearance, such as the squirrel, woolly and spider monkeys. Also included are howler monkeys, one of the largest New World monkeys, weighing up to sixteen and a half pounds. The size and shape of their lower jaw help the howler produce loud cries and deep howls heard two to three miles away!

The Colobus monkey is an Old World monkey.

OLD WORLD MONKEYS

These are monkeys that inhabit parts of Africa, Asia, Japan and the East Indies. ("Old World" is a term used for the eastern hemisphere.) They are different from the New World monkeys in that they have nostrils that are close together and open to the front, like human nostrils do. If these monkeys have tails they are not prehensile; if they have thumbs they are opposable.

Male species in this family may have very large canines for eating small animals. There are two groups, or sub-families, of Old World monkeys. One includes the guenons, macaques and baboons that have cheek pouches, a long or short tail, and five digits on their hands.

The other subfamily— the langurs, and several monkeys such as the Colobus monkey—have tails (with a few exceptions) but no cheek pouches. They often do not have thumbs, but if they have them, they are very small.

Many of the Old World monkeys have delightful caps, beards and head crests. Another species, the proboscis monkey, is obviously well named because its nose may hang down below its mouth!

The baboon, an Old World monkey, has nostrils that are close together and open towards the front.

APES

Apes include gibbons, chimpanzees, orangutans and gorillas. A major noticeable difference between apes and monkeys is that apes lack a tail. Apes' arms are longer than their bodies and they use them to swing through the trees. Apes swing below the branches while monkeys run along the branches.

LESSER APE or GIBBON

Gibbons are called the lesser apes because they are smaller than great apes. They are very agile with their long arms that may be twice as long as their slender bodies. They swing through the trees and can even leap 40 feet from branch to branch! For added traveling ease, they can use their hands as "hooks" because their thumbs connect near the wrist instead of the palm.

The acrobatic gibbons live in Southeast Asia. They are highly arboreal and rarely descend to the ground. But when they do, it has been said they look like tightrope walkers because they keep their hands over their heads for balance.

The gibbon is considered a brachiator because its long arms (*brachio* means arm) can support and propel its body.

GREAT APE

The family of great apes includes orangutans, chimpanzees and gorillas. This family has a large braincase and so is quite intelligent. Gorillas and chimpanzees resemble each other in form and live in social groups more often than the orangutans.

Gorillas are the largest of all primates, weighing up to 400 pounds. They have muscular, stocky bodies, short muzzles and large nostrils. Chimpanzees are more arboreal than gorillas. In addition to eating plant material, the chimps may also eat small mammals.

The orangutan, sometimes called "old man of the forest" has facial features such as a bulging snout and cheek pads. Like the other great apes, the orangutan's diet consists mainly of plant material but may also consist of birds or eggs.

Chimpanzee

HUMAN BEINGS

This is where scientists classify us. We belong right in the midst of all the other primates because we share more characteristics with the primates than with any other mammal.

But the big difference with us is our amazingly big brains that allow us to create and make choices, unlike any other animal. We can live almost anywhere because of our mobility, ability to create complex shelters (we can use tools well), and ability to regulate low temperatures (by fire and clothing).

Homo sapiens are also brachiators.

RODENTS
GNAWING MAMMALS
(to the tune of "The E-ri-e")

Two popular songs that were sung by the work crews on the Erie Canal are still remembered: "The Erie Canal" and "The E-ri-e."

Unknown   Lyrics by Dorry Eldon

Squir - rel, rat and por - cu - pine ro - dents are the gnaw - ing

kind there's lots of plac- es where we find mam - mals of the gnaw - ing kind.

They move their jaw from front to back as they chew their food at - tack

in - ci - sor teeth that al - ways grow they must gnaw to keep them so low.

Chorus

They are mam - mals ve - ry small they are the most nu - merous of all.

There's a - bout one thou - sand six hun - dred nine - ty spe - cies por -

cu - pine, squir - rel, and rat- like, are sub - or - ders a - mong these.

They've got a space behind their incisor teeth
Some have pouches in their cheeks
But they grind with their cheek teeth
Beavers they can change a creek
Chisel teeth they use to bite
On our crops they are blight
Quickly multiply, a fright
Nocturnal some move at night
Chorus

Porcupine-like include nutria
Capybara and chinchilla
Rat-like are most rats and mice
Hamsters, lemmings, and the dormice
Squirrel-like are the prairie dog,
Chipmunk, beaver and groundhog
Squirrels of course and gophers too
Mice: only pocket and kangaroo
Chorus

RODENTS
GNAWING MAMMALS

The rodents are by far the largest order of mammals. As of the latest classification there are 29 families, 380 genera and 1,687 species! Rodents live in all kinds of places, some live in the ground, such as groundhogs or marmots; some live in trees, such as squirrels; while others are semiaquatic, such as beavers. Rodents move by running, leaping, climbing and some, like the flying squirrel, can even glide.

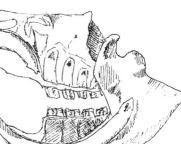

A beaver jaw shows large, ever-growing incisors and the **diastema**, traits of all rodents.

A major characteristic of rodents is their four (two above, two below) large incisor teeth used for gnawing hard objects in a front-to-back motion. The incisors' outer surface is harder than the inner surface; this makes the teeth chisel-like. The incisors are also ever-growing, which means they will grow throughout the rodent's life and become too long if the rodent does not continually wear them down.

Behind the incisors there is a large space where canine teeth in humans, and in carnivores, grow. This space, called the **diastema**, allows the rodents to use their gnawing teeth to full advantage without the animals' tongue getting in the way.

Rodents also have grinding cheek teeth; in some species they are also ever-growing. Rodents also need to grind their back teeth on hard objects, such as nuts and seeds, to keep them in good condition. If the rodent's diet is soft, both incisors and cheek teeth may continue growing right through the roof of the mouth, and the lower teeth in front of the nose!

Some rodents have cheek pouches either inside or outside their mouths to help these small animals carry large amounts of food. The external fur-lined pouches, such as those of the pocket gopher, can even be turned inside out for cleaning! Hamsters and chipmunks have the inside type of cheek pouches and can fill them to near bursting.

The doctor comforts and prepares a little guinea pig for surgery.

Kingdom : Animal
Phylum: Vertebrata
Class: Mammal
Order: Rodentia
Family: Caviidae
Genus: *Cavia*
Species: *porcellus*

Scientific name:
 Cavia porcellus
Common name:
 Guinea pig

Some rodents, such as the prairie dogs, are very social creatures and live in large groups. They are called dogs because they can make barking sounds.

To help further classify such a large order, characteristics of the jaw and structures in the skull are used to separate rodents into three suborders.

1- **Squirrel-like rodents**
2- **Rat-like rodents**
3- **Porcupine-like rodents**

Squirrel

SQUIRREL-LIKE RODENTS
This suborder of squirrel-like rodents includes the squirrels, of course, and other rodents such as marmots, prairie dogs, chipmunks, pocket gophers, springhares and mountain and true beavers. Only a few of the many, many families are described below.

Squirrels, Chipmunks, Marmots, Prairie Dogs
This family includes about 250 different species that live almost anywhere in the world except Australia, Egypt, southern South America and Madagascar. Most are **diurnal** (active during the day) and eat nuts and seeds, though a few species eat insects and small animals.

The smallest squirrel, the African Pygmy Squirrel, is only 5 inches and the largest is the Indian Giant of 3 feet in length. Squirrel genera include the following.

Chipmunk

Ground Squirrels rarely climb trees but live in burrows in the ground. They live in prairies, tundra, steppes, woodlands and desert mountains. Some species hibernate. **Tree Squirrels** live in trees, as their name implies, but gather food on the ground.

Red Squirrels or Chickarees live in trees but spend much time on the ground. These are squirrels that will eat eggs, baby rabbits, or mice in addition to nuts and seeds. **Flying Squirrels** can glide downward from high branches using the skin between their arms and legs. Though they do not actually fly, they can glide up to one third of a mile and bank and rise before landing on a branch.

Ground hogs (also called woodchucks)
are large squirrel-like rodents weighing up to 17 pounds. They nearly double their weight just before hibernation because they sleep 7 to 8 months!—The longest hibernation of any animal. February 2 is Goundhog's Day; if a groundhog comes out of its burrow, sees its shadow and returns to its burrow, will there be a late spring?

How much wood could a woodchuck chuck, if a woodchuck could chuck wood?

Pocket Gophers have cheek pouches on the outside of their mouths. They may live in deserts, prairies, meadows, open forests and perhaps even your garden. The gopher's name comes from a word meaning "honeycomb" because it makes tunnels in all directions until the ground is like a honeycomb. The gopher's tunneling is distinct from that of the mole because it does not leave ridges on the ground surface.

Pocket gophers have external cheek pouches.

Pocket Mice, Kangaroo Rats, Kangaroo Mice

comprise over 60 species that live in North and Central America and the northern part of South America. Their habitat ranges from desert to tropical forest. They travel by jumping because their hind legs are much longer than their short front legs.

Mountain beavers, also called **sewellels,** are not beavers nor do they love the mountains! Sewellels have heavy, tailless bodies with short limbs and front feet that are good for digging. They live near water in forest or thickets, and eat plant material, including bark, if other food is not available. Mountain beavers do not hibernate.

A beaver has been here!

Beavers are considered the lumberjacks, builders and engineers of the forest. They work hard making dams to create ponds for their homes. They fell trees by gnawing around their bases but they also dig canals to get those trees to the dams. They roll, drag or push the log to the canal and float it into place in the dam. With beavers' characteristic efficiency, smaller branches are pulled to a food pile and are added to the shelter and dam after the bark has been eaten off.

The beaver builds its lodge of stick and mud in a pond for protection. The dam provides the still deep waters necessary for it.

The beaver is one of the largest rodents and has a thick, strong body useful for all its many heavy tasks. It is a good swimmer because its hind feet are webbed; its tail can turn almost on its edge, acting as a rudder for steering. The beaver can easily stay underwater for five minutes but has been recorded staying below the surface for a full 15 minutes!

The beaver played a large role in the history and development of Canada and the United States. Trappers moved westward in search of the popular beaver pelt used for making hats and coats. Settlements grew around areas the trappers met for rendezvous and towns began to form.

The beaver can weigh up to 50 lbs. and grow to 4 feet, including its tail.

RAT-LIKE RODENTS

The family with the most species of the entire mammal class belongs to the suborder of rat-like rodents. It is the family of **murids** which includes over 1,000 species! These rodents live in all kinds of habitats worldwide, and reproduce at prolific rates. Murids include species such as mice, rats, hamsters, voles, and lemmings. Rodents are an important part of the food chain, supplying carnivores with a constant source of meat.

Mice include both house and wild species. They look like small rats with their long noses, long skinny tails and round ears. The pygmy mouse can be as small as two inches long and weigh only one-fourth ounce; that is about the same weight as a gluestick!

Rats can grow to almost 2 feet long and weigh up to 15 pounds! They are usually larger than mice and have a characteristic long pointed nose and long tail. Rats live in varied habitats, but the brown ("Norway") and the black ("roof") rats, often live near people. These rats have been carriers of diseases such as Bubonic Plague, typhus and Rocky Mountain spotted fever.

The wood rat is also called the trader rat because it drops whatever it is carrying when it sees something else it wants. It especially likes shiny objects, and its nest is said to hold coins, glass, and even silverware!

Dwarf hamsters and golden hamsters are two kinds of popular little pets native to Mongolia, Siberia, Manchuria and Eastern Europe. In the wild or in captivity they fill their cheek pouches with plant material and seeds to the point of bursting.

Voles are the size of heavyset, large mice but are distinguished by their blunt noses. They have tails that are shorter than their body, sometimes only half its length. Voles are the fastest breeders, bearing ten young at one time, with ten litters a year! Some species of voles are commonly called meadow mice.

Lemmings have small, stocky bodies and thick fur for the cold northern tundra and alpine regions where they live. They multiply prolifically, and thousands migrate together when their communities grow too large and their food runs out. They run through the mountains

Just a few of the rat-like species include:

Rice rat
Water rat
Climbing rat
Big-eared climbing rat
Vesper rat
Andean rat
Water rat
Crimson-nosed rat
Swamp rat
Coney rat
Marsh rat
Cotton rat
Pack rat
Wood rat
Aquatic rat

Crested rat
Andean swamp rat
Chilean rat
White-tailed rat
African mole-rat
Blind mole-rat
Zokors
Voalavoanala
Karroo rat
Bamboo rat
Fat sand rat
Monkey-footed rat
Tree rat
Puna mouse
Brown mice
Red-nosed mouse
Burrowing mice
Harvest mouse
Pericotes
Andean mouse
Climbing mouse
Deer mice
Golden mouse
Pygmy mouse
Grasshopper mouse
Grass mice
Field mice
Cane mice
Shrew mice
Tree mice
Gerbil mice

Fat mice
Rock mice
Swamp mouse
Mole mice
Vesper mice
Rato-do-Mato
Leaf-eared mice
Chinchilla mouse
Dwarf hamster
Mouselike hamster
Black-bellied hamster
Rat-like hamster

Golden hamster
Spiny dormouse
Chinese pygmy dormouse
Northern pygmy gerbil
Southern pygmy gerbil
Short-tailed gerbil
Large naked-soled gerbil
Small naked-soled gerbil
Fat-tailed gerbil
Przewalski's gerbil
Great gerbil
Walo
Jird
Bushy-tailed jird
Bank vole
Pratt's vole
High mountain vole

Martino's snow vole
Water vole
Pine vole
Muskrat
True lemming
Wood lemming
Bog lemming
Collared lemming [2]
Etc., etc., etc.!

From Walker's Mammals of the World 4th Edition.

and may swim through rivers until they reach an area rich in plant material. Carnivores can have a feast during lemmings' migratory journeys!

Muskrats are the largest members of the rat family and have been hunted and trapped in North America for their dense, glossy fur. The muskrat gets its name from its musky smell. It is a good swimmer with its webbed hind feet and flattened tail for a rudder.

Dormice may look like squirrels or chipmunks because of their bushy tails, but dormice are much smaller.

PORCUPINE-LIKE RODENTS

The porcupine-like rodents are a diverse group that include all rodent families that do not fit into the squirrel or rat-like rodent suborders. Some families include the following species.

Porcupine
A baby porcupine is called a porcupette.

New World Porcupines have very few enemies and are usually left alone because of their long barbed quills. One dangerous enemy is the fisher, who knows how to flip a porcupine on its back to get the quill-less underparts. If other animals unwisely attack the porcupine the four-inch quills detach and may become embedded in the flesh, causing infection and even death.

Chinchilla

The porcupine has a thick, heavy body with an arched back. It walks cumbersomely along with the whole foot on the ground. It is a good tree climber with rough foot pads and sharp claws to help it grip trees. Porcupines can weigh up to 40 pounds and be 3 feet long. A porcupette is a baby porcupine.

Chinchillas have very dense, soft fur for the cold weather of the high Andes in South America. The fur is the most valuable kind for its size and weight—there may be as many as 60 1-inch hairs growing from each hair follicle!

The quills are hollow, and there can be 30,000 of them in some species! Many New World porcupines have quills that are 4 inches long but an Old World species has quills that are 15 inches long!

Some of the commonly known porcupine-like species are:

New World porcupines
Old World porcupines
Cavies
Guinea pigs
Nutria
Chinchilla
Capybara

Chinchillas have large ears and eyes, blue-gray fur and long, bushy tails.

Capybaras are the largest rodents growing to 4 feet long and weighing up to 120 pounds! They are also called water pigs because they are good swimmers, live near the water and look like big guinea pigs. Capybaras live in South America, east of the Andes between Panama and Paraguay.

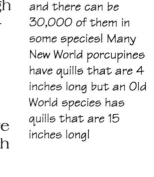

Capybara

RODENT-LIKE MAMMALS
(to the tune of "Irish Washerwoman")

One of the most well-known and popular Irish jigs is "Irish Washerwoman." It is usually played as a fiddle tune and whenever anyone puts words to it, it always becomes a quick-moving tongue twister.

Unknown   Lyrics by Dorry Eldon

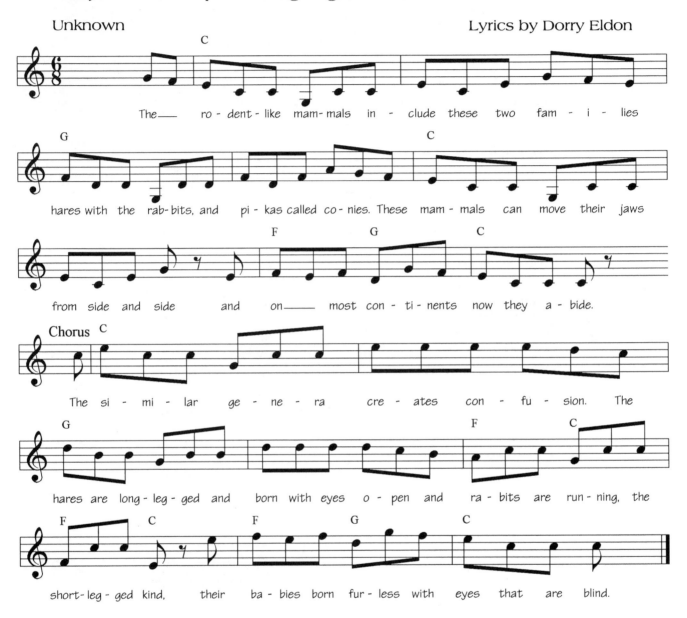

The— ro - dent - like mam- mals in - clude these two fam - i - lies

hares with the rab- bits, and pi - kas called co - nies. These mam - mals can move their jaws

from side and side and on—— most con - ti - nents now they a - bide.

Chorus

The si - mi - lar ge - ne - ra cre - ates con - fu - sion. The

hares are long - leg - ged and born with eyes o - pen and ra - bits are run - ning, the

short- leg - ged kind, their ba - bies born fur - less with eyes that are blind.

They've four incisor teeth on jaws that are upper
The hare is the species that is a high jumper
The family of pikas are animals small
They have short, broad ears and no tails at all
Chorus

All lagomorphs eat in herbivorous habit
The hares have long ears and include the jackrabbit
And rabbits include those whose tails are small:
The domestic rabbit and cottontails all
Chorus

RODENT-LIKE MAMMALS

The order **lagomorpha** includes two herbivorous families: the pikas (also called conies) and the rabbits and hares. These mammals live nearly anywhere. Australia and parts of southern South America are the only places where they are not **indigenous**, or native, to the area.

Kingdom : Animal
Phylum: Vertebrata
Class: Mammal
Order: Lagomorpha
Family: Leporidae
Genus: *Sylvilagus*
Species: *floridanus*

Scientific name:
  Sylvilagus floridanus
Common name:
  Eastern cottontail

The species of this order can resemble rodents. They also share jaw similarities in that they have ever-growing incisors and the diastema. But lagomorphs' teeth and jaws are different in the following ways.
  1- They have four incisor teeth on the upper jaw (rodents have two).
  2- They grind their food in a side-to-side jaw motion (rodents gnaw front to back).

PIKAS

Pikas are small tailless animals of about six inches in length. With their short, broad ears they look more like rodents than rabbits or hares. They also cannot jump or run as fast and so do not venture far from their homes.

The little pikas live in community groups and are known for making "hay." That is, they bite off grasses and other plants and let them dry in the sun. Then they take the hay to their burrows where it is stacked in piles to be eaten during the winter months. In Russia, pika hay piles can weigh up to 44 pounds![3]

Some pika species live in mountains of the western United States, and parts of Alaska. They make their homes among large rocks or boulders in alpine areas where nearby grasses supply their hay.

Other pikas live in eastern Europe, Asia, Pakistan, India and Burma. These kinds live in various habitats of open plains, forests and desert-steppes.

Pikas are also called the crying or whistling hares because they use their voices. Hares and rabbits do not make noises except when totally terrified—then they make a blood-curdling scream and often die from shock, even if physically unharmed!

Eastern cottontail
All cottontails are rabbits.

RABBITS and HARES
This family, which includes both rabbits and hares, has been extremely successful in adapting to different habitats. Cottontails, in particular, can be found almost everywhere in the United States. Some species are excellent swimmers and live semiaquatic lives! These little animals are actually strong competitors with other animals for similar food and shelter because they can multiply so quickly.

Rabbits and hares share general similarities such as the ability to hop, relatively long ears and similar habitats. They are further classified into different genera by other specific characteristics such as actual ear length, the way they move and the places they live. Common names often do not give a clue to which genera the animals belong—some species, such as the jackrabbit and the snowshoe rabbit are not rabbits but hares!

Newborn rabbits are
born furless and blind.

RABBITS
Rabbits are the cuddly-looking, bunny-type species such as the cottontails. They are distinct from hares in that they have:
 1- shorter ears.
 2- shorter legs for running, not jumping.
 3- babies that are born furless and blind.

Rabbits do not have the long legs nor the speed required to escape their enemies, so they usually feed close to their homes. To escape, they hide in thick cover or in burrows. Groups living together in burrows are called **warrens**.

HARES
Simply stated, hares are the lanky, wild-looking species. They tend to be larger than rabbits and live on the surface of the land rather than in burrows. Their other distinguishing features include:
 1- long ears.
 2- long legs for jumping.
 3- babies that are born with fur and sight.

The hares usually escape their enemies by sheer speed. When jackrabbits are pursued, they bound in leaps of 15 to 20 feet with speeds up to 40 miles per hour! They often make their homes in the grass of open fields, and do not need to hide from carnivores because they can outrun them.

Newborn hares are
born with fur and sight.

Hare

Some of the most common hares are the snowshoe rabbit, the European hare and the jackrabbit. The North American jackrabbits need little water and can feed on almost any kind of vegetation.

Sometimes jackrabbits' ears can grow up to one-third of the hares' length—the antelope jackrabbits' ears may grow to eight inches long! The blood flow in the ears cools hares down like a car radiator cools an engine. These ears also give hares a keen sense of hearing. They depend on it for protection from nearby carnivores hungry for a bite of meat.

The snowshoe rabbit, or varying hare, has a fur coat that changes with the seasons: it is white in the winter and brown in the summer.

As mentioned earlier, hares and rabbits are adaptable to different habitats. European hares were introduced in Australia and have been so successful that they have caused the extinction or near extinction of some native marsupials. Lethal viruses have been purposefully developed and have been successful in helping control the hare population on that continent.

The phrase "mad as a March hare" is often found in literature. It refers to the behavior of males during the early spring when they leap and tumble before mating.

Hares and rabbits are prolific reproducers: another characteristic to their success at survival. Though they can run fast and hide well, they supply a rich food source for the wild carnivore population.

BATS
(to the tune of "Take Me Out to the Ball Game")

"Take Me Out to the Ball Game" will live forever in Americans hearts! The words were written in 1908 by Albert van Tilzer, supposedly twenty years before he saw his first ball game!

Albert von Tilzer   Lyrics by Dorry Eldon

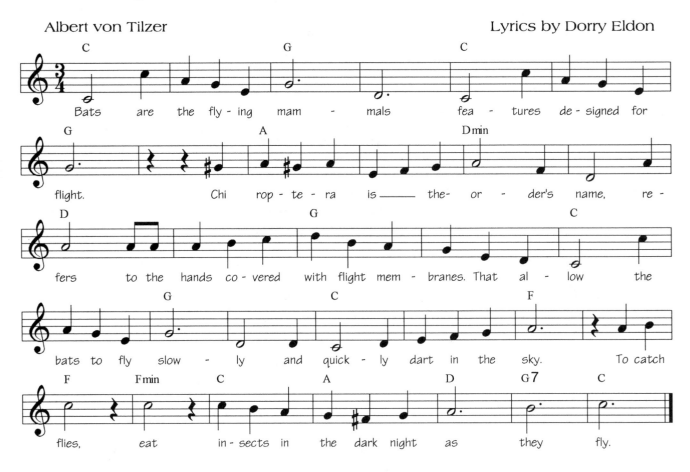

Bats are the fly-ing mam - mals fea - tures de - signed for flight. Chi rop - te - ra is ___ the- or - der's name, re - fers to the hands co - vered with flight mem - branes. That al - low the bats to fly slow - ly and quick - ly dart in the sky. To catch flies, eat in - sects in the dark night as they fly.

Nearly a thousand species
And bats can navigate well
Most use a method that's like radar
Echolocation to know where things are
For they can squeak very high pitches
That bounce off the objects nearby
And return to them as an echo as they fly

Bats disperse seeds of fruit trees,
Others pollinate plants
Insect control to the humans give
Bats return at dawn to the places they live
In the caves or up in the treetops
To hang upside down by their feet
And the bats are really so helpful to man and beast

BATS

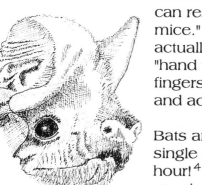

There are nearly 1000 species of bats—that's more than any other order except rodents. And because they can resemble rodents, the German name means "flying mice." Bats, though, are the only mammals that actually fly. The order's name, chiroptera, meaning "hand wing," describes how they fly: the elongated fingers have a flight membrane stretching over them and across the back.

Bats are beneficial in controlling insect populations. A single little brown bat can eat 600 mosquitoes in one hour![4] They are also beneficial for pollinating wild plant species and dispersing the seeds of wild tropical fruit and nut trees. Many of these plant species are dependent on bats for their survival. Unfortunately for plants and people, bats do not reproduce like rodents—they have only one baby, called a pup, per year.

Bats are covered with fine fur, except the unusual naked bat. In fact, bats have some of the finest hair of any mammal—1,500,000 hairs per square inch!

Kingdom : Animal
Phylum: Vertebrata
Class: Mammal
Order: Chiroptera
Family: Molossidae
Genus: *Nytinomops*
Species: *femorosaccus*

Scientific name:
   Nytinomops femorosaccus
Common name:
   Pocketed free-tail bat

Spotted bat

Because the order has so many species with so many different eating habits, it is helpful to distinguish them according to their diet.

> **1- Insect-eating** bats include 70% of all bat species and are usually small in size.
> **2- Fruit-eating** bats are large bats that live in the warm tropics.
> **3- Nectar, pollen** or **flower-eating** bats are very small.
> **4- Meat-eating** bats include those that eat frogs, lizards, small birds, mice, or fish. (Fish-eating bats have little cheek pouches.)
> **5- Blood-eating** bats are the vampire bats of Latin America (not Transylvania!).

The membrane is really an extension of the skin on the back and belly that continues out to the legs and tail. The membrane's thickness is said to be comparable to that of plastic wrap! Bats have four fingers and one thumb on each hand. The short thumb, with its sharp claw, holds onto the places where the bat lands.

Scientifically, bats are classified into two suborders depending upon such physical features as the size of their eyes, size of their ears and their main food source.

MEGACHIROPTERA or OLD WORLD FRUIT BATS

As their name implies, these are the mega- or large bats: they weigh up to 4 pounds, with wing spans up to nearly 6 feet! These bats are also called **flying foxes** because of their distinctive fox-like faces. In comparison to bats in the other suborder, these bats have smaller ears and very large eyes. Some species' eyesight is believed to be 10 times better than humans'!

Franquet's flying fox
Megabats are born with thick hair and open eyes.

These species are fruit- or flower-eaters and use their keen sense of smell and sight to find their food. Fruit-eaters can cause crop damage for tropical fruit growers, but they also play an important role in wild plant propagation as they spread seeds from the fruits they eat.

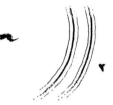

Most Old World bats live in tropical climates of Africa, Australia, Asia and islands in the Pacific and Indian Oceans.

MICROCHIROPTERA or NEW WORLD BATS

All other species of bats belong to the largest suborder, the microbats. There is wide variety in their diets—although most eat insects, others eat nectar, lizards, small birds, fish, rodents, or mammal blood.

False vampire
Microbats are born hairless with their eyes closed.

These small bats have large ears and small eyes, often the size of pinheads. Nocturnal animals usually have large eyes to see at night, but these bats depend on **echolocation** instead of sight to find their food. They emit high-pitched sounds through their nose or mouth that bounce off nearby objects and insects. The sounds come back to the bat as echoes, which the bat uses to guide it through the dark.

Many microbats have unusual noses and scientists think they are used for echolocation. Their distinctive looks are often the basis for their common names: bulldog, hog-nosed, leaf-nosed, horseshoe, trident-nosed (with three little spears), tube-nosed, hammer-headed and even spear- and sword-nosed.

Echolocation:
The bat emits a high-pitched sound that bounces off insects or other objects to help the bat locate its food.

Flower- or nectar-eaters have long snouts and very long tongues. Because they feed on the pollen and nectar of flowers, they are also helpful in plant pollination. Grains of pollen stick to their long snouts and are transferred to other plants as the bats feed. Some plants, such as the desert saguaro and other cacti, depend on bats instead of bees for pollination.

Most species of bats live in tropical and temperate climates, but there are those that need to prepare for winter. Some bats, such as the Mexican free-tail, migrate 800 –1600 miles to warmer winter climates. Some hibernate, such as the little brown bats. When they do, their bodies become the same temperature as the environment around them, even though they are warmblooded! They need to be careful to find caves or other shelters where the temperature will not get too cold, or it could kill them!

Bat handlers report that bats are shy and gentle and even come when they are called! They say bats show their affection to them by licking their hand or cheek.

The largest colony of bats in the world is in Bracken Cave, Texas where there are as many as 20 million bats. Each night they eat 250 tons of insects! [5]

INSECTIVORES
(to the tune of "Camptown Races")

Today, "Camptown Races" ranks just below "Oh Susanna" as the most popular Stephen Foster song. During its early years it was not successful and made its composer little money.

Stephen Foster   Lyrics by Dorry Eldon

In - sec - ti - vores are al - so called the in - sect eat-ers. They in - clude hedge - hog and shrew, and so - le - no - don too. There are six fam - i - lies, four hun - dred six spe - cies with ten - rec and the gold - en mole, al - so the "true" mole.

Here's some common traits among these insect-eaters:
Good sense of smell is what you'll find with species of this kind
Their eyes can be so small, not much use at all
And with their snouts so long and thin the ground they burrow in

A hedgehog's not a porcupine but an insect-eater
It is not hard to define, it has barbless spines
Most roll into a ball, if afraid at all
The porcupine so large and fat cannot roll up like that

The smallest mammal that is found is an insect-eater
It is called the pygmy shrew; they can eat meat too
Some can eat their weight in food every day
But elephant and tree shrew now have their own orders too

INSECTIVORES

Species in this order eat insects, as their name rightly implies, though some may eat small animals and birds. The deciding factor in classification is not a diet of insects, otherwise the anteater and armadillo would be included.

Shrew jaw

Insectivore species are mammals that are very, very small. They have long, narrow snouts, small brains, small·ears, and sometimes extremely small eyes. There are six families of insectivores.

> **1- Hedgehogs** have barbless spines and can roll into a ball when threatened.
> **2- Shrews** are small with big appetites.
> **3- Solenodons** are shrew-like but larger.
> **4- Tenrecs** may resemble hedgehogs, mice, shrews, or even otters.
> **5- Moles** have front feet that turn out for digging and have five digits on each paw.
> **6- Golden moles** are similar to true moles except for their coloration and four, instead of five, digits on their paws.

HEDGEHOGS

Hedgehogs are common insectivores on the British Isles and have long been dearly loved fixtures in young children's literature. The real animals are covered with barbless spines (porcupines are barbed). When threatened, they can roll themselves into a ball.

Unlike many insectivores, hedgehogs have well-developed eyes and ears. They use them to hunt insects, their main food, as well as frogs, snakes and young birds. Hedgehogs are good swimmers and climbers but are terrestrial mammals. They usually dig their own burrows and live alone in them except during breeding and raising of young.

Kingdom : Animal
Phylum: Vertebrata
Class: Mammal
Order: Insectivora
Family: Erinaceidae
Genus: *Erinaceus*
Species: *europaeus*

Scientific name:
  Erinaceus europaeus
Common name:
  Eurasian hedgehog

Hedgehogs live in many different climates of Europe, Africa and Asia. When they have been taken to other parts of the world, they have thrived as gentle pets, in spite of their barbs.

The hedgehog is about 12 inches long.

SHREWS

The shrew family is large, found world wide and consists of 250 species. Included are the water shrew, the long-tailed shrew and the pygmy shrew. Most shrews have the appearance of a long-nosed mouse, and are often mistaken for one. Shrews are not rodents but vicious, fierce-fighting (sometimes with poisonous bites) insectivores.

The tree shrew is not considered a shrew, nor an insectivore, but is classified in its own order! See single-family orders, p. 77.

Many species of shrew babies travel connected to each other and to their mother—they won't get lost unless they fall off or let go!

Though these mammals are small, they eat vast amounts of food for their size. Many eat their own weight in food every day—but the little pygmy shrew can even eat three times its weight every day! Shrews' voracious appetites inspired a classic Hollywood horror film called *Attack of the Giant Shrews*. (Gigantic hungry shrews hunt for their next meal on an island where stranded people are desperate to get off.)

Fortunately, very fortunately, most shrews are small. The pygmy shrew, the smallest land mammal (ties with the bumblebee bat for the smallest mammal) weighs only .05 –.07 ounces and measures 1 inch without its tail. *Walker's Mammals of the World* helps us understand the size of the tiny pygmy shrew:

> *The pygmy shrew is so small that its insect-like holes in leaf mold are not quite large enough to admit a pencil. It can travel in the tunnel of large beetles.*[6]

Approximate size of the pygmy shrew.

All shrews have a keen sense of hearing, and some may even hunt by echolocation as do bats and porpoises. Shrews give off high-pitched sounds that hit objects and bounce back, telling them exactly where to find their prey.

SOLENODONS

The solenodon is one of the least-known insectivores, perhaps because it lives only in Haiti and Cuba. It looks like a large shrew, but is about twelve inches long and weighs about two pounds. It is often mistaken for a long-nosed rat.

Like the shrew, solenodons may hunt by echolocation and poison their next meal with a deadly bite.

TENREC

Tenrecs are also another little-known insectivore family. They inhabit parts of Africa, but are mainly found on the island of Madagascar and nearby Comoro Islands. Some with spiny hair resemble hedgehogs, while others look like shrews. There is even an aquatic species called the otter shrew which, as the name implies, is otter-like in appearance. It has a long body, flattened tail and dense fur. It is one of the largest insectivores.

TRUE MOLE

A medieval name for moles means "earth throwers." The mole's snout is long and slender, a good tool for pushing and shoving soil. A mole's legs are short and each foot has five digits. The large front feet are turned outward making them very useful for digging away at the soil.

The classic book *The Wind in the Willows* features a little mole wearing glasses because, of course, real moles have very poor eyesight. The eyes are often hidden in the thick fur, but are unnecessary to a life underground. Instead, the mole uses its keen sense of vibrations for locating food and traveling through the earth.

Moles make two types of tunnels. One is shallow with a ridge of soil marking a path as the mole's back pushes up the soil. These tunnels are for resting and feeding. The other type of tunnel is deep and usually marked by a molehill where the mole has pushed the soil out. These deep tunnels are for sheltering the mole and its young.

The common mole is only five to six inches long. The mole usually lives alone, but there are Old World species that dig communities and tunnels for up to 40 moles.

The mole has velvety, thick fur.

Moleskin was once very popular in the 1800s. In one year, England sent 4 million moleskins to America to be used for jackets and coats!

GOLDEN MOLES

The golden moles are so named because of their unusual coloring of yellow, bronze, or red. They are like the true moles, except they have four digits on their front paw unlike the true moles' five.

"TOOTHLESS" MAMMALS

(to the tune of "Yellow Rose of Texas")

"The Yellow Rose of Texas" was a popular song in the 1860s. No one knows who wrote it but the first published manuscript bears the initials J. K. The song was popular throughout the South, especially with Texas troops during the Civil War.

Unknown   Lyrics by Dorry Eldon

Ar - ma - dil - los live in Tex - as, south of the bor - der too con - si - dered "tooth-less" mam-mals, ant - eat - er and sloth too the ant - eat - er eats the in - sects and worms found in the ground the sloth likes to hang on the trees and view things up - side down.

The order's edentata, with creatures so diverse
Of course they are all mammals 'cause their babies, mothers nurse
Because the sloth lives in the trees, it is arboreal
Armadillos 'n anteaters that live on the land are terrestrial

The anteater's mouth is but a small hole of pencil size
Its sense of smell is keen 'cause it can't rely on its eyes
It finds an ant nest digs a bit and then inserts its snout
It uses its long sticky tongue to pull the insects out

Armadillos can defend themselves by their protective plates
That are skin-covered bone, this is the armadillo's trait
The tree sloth climbs from limb to limb its movement is so slow
But it can hardly walk at all if on the ground below

"TOOTHLESS" MAMMALS

The Latin name for the order, *edentata*, means "toothless ones." The teeth of species that even have them are unusually small and lack the hard outside layer, or enamel, found on other mammals' teeth. The order includes three very diverse families: armadillos, anteaters and sloths.

The anteater is the only family without teeth, while another family species, the giant armadillo, has up to 100 small, peg-like teeth—that's more than any other mammal! But these teeth are shed as the animal grows.

Families of the edentates live in Central and South America and the southern tip of North America. In addition to the lack of true mammal-like teeth, these animals share additional characteristics, including:
> **1-** long skulls with small brains.
> **2-** very large and long middle claws on their forelimbs.
> **3-** an extra articulation, or movable part called a **xenarthrale**, gives the hips extra support. The order is sometimes called xenarthrales, for this specific unique feature.

> The families' teeth:
> Anteater: No teeth
> Armadillo: Bare gums
>   in front; few peg-
>   like teeth in back.
> Sloth: Bare gums
>   in front, few peg-
>   like teeth in back.

The three-banded armadillo can roll itself into a tight ball to protect itself from enemies.

Kingdom :	Animal
Phylum:	Vertebrata
Class:	Mammal
Order:	Edentata
Family:	Dasypodidae
Genus:	*Tolypeutes*
Species:	*tricinctus*

Scientific name:
  Tolypeutes tricinctus
Common name:
  Three-banded armadillo

ARMADILLOS

The distinctive feature of the armadillos is their protective armor-like coat. "Armadillo" comes from the Spanish word meaning "little armored one." The armor-like covering consists of bands of horn and bone connected with flexible skin. Armadillos come in all sizes: from the pink fairy species of only 7 inches, to the 4-foot giant weighing 130 pounds.

The head and legs are covered with shields and the legs can also be drawn up next to the body inside the main protective armor. Armadillos' stomachs are vulnerable areas, but they have several other ways to protect themselves by:
> **1-** Burrowing quickly into the ground, enough to hide their belly, leaving only the armor exposed.
> **2-** Curling themselves up. Only one species, the three-banded armadillo, can roll itself into a tight ball. When it does, nothing can unroll it.
> **3-** Leaping three feet straight up into the air! This startles predators and may even dislocate hungry jaws by the force of the blow.

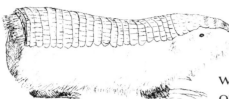

Armadillos' front legs have powerful claws with three, four or five digits depending upon the species; the back legs have five. Armadillos usually walk on the tips of their claws (!) and soles of their feet.

The pink fairy armadillo has a flat armor plate on its rear that it can use to plug the opening of its burrow.

Armadillos have good hearing and a keen sense of smell, and use these senses to find food. The nine-banded armadillo has such a fine sense of smell that it can locate worms and insects buried eight inches in the ground! Armadillos' tongues are covered with wart-like bumps and sticky saliva that help them catch their main food source—insects. In addition, armadillos may eat plants, small animals, eggs and **carrion** (dead animals).

ANTEATERS

Anteaters are not classified in the order of insectivores, but they certainly know how to eat insects—anteaters can eat 30,000 ants or termites in a day! They have several features similar to the armadillo for doing this.

1- Good sense of smell for locating prey, usually an ant nest.

2- Long, powerful claws to dig and break through the ant nest's thick walls.

3- Tongues, with wart-like bumps like the armadillo's, become coated with sticky saliva when catching and eating insects.

There are three genera of anteaters: the giant, that may grow to 5 feet long and weigh over 80 pounds; the lesser, or tamanduas; and the smallest, the silky anteater, that lives in trees.

The claws are also powerful for protection and the anteater will use them if necessary. The giant anteater even walks on the sides of its paws to protect them! Different species of anteaters may have two to four fingers on the front legs, and four to five toes on the hind legs.

Anteaters do not have teeth— insects are digested by the stomach.

The anteater has a characteristic long, narrow snout with a pencil-shaped mouth. It has poor hearing and eyesight. It lives in tropical forests, savannas, and swampy areas in Central and South America.

SLOTHS

The seven species of sloths are
divided into two genera according
to the number of toes— there are
two-toed and three-toed sloths. All
species live in trees of Central and
South America, where they eat
leaves, twigs, buds and fruit.

Sloths have long claws that hook onto
branches to help these arboreal creatures
hang upside down. They may even
remain hooked when dead! They have
never been seriously hunted because
when they are shot and killed, they do not
even fall to the ground!

The sloth's claws can
be almost 3 inches long!

Sloths are as suited for living in the trees as whales
are suited for the ocean. If sloths descend to the
ground, they cannot walk. They have difficulty
standing and can only drag themselves along
because their legs cannot support their weight.

Sloths sleep almost all the time—18 hours a day.
When they are awake, they are extremely slow
movers. Moving 15 feet in one minute, they are the
slowest mammals in the world. Their slow
movements, sleeping habits, and the moist, warm
climate of their habitat allow algae to grow on their fur.
Their fur may even have a green cast to it! The fur is
parted on the belly of the sloth to help it shed water
as it hangs upside down.

Sloths have a poor sense of hearing but keen senses
of smell and touch. They have good eyesight and can
turn their head to look in almost any direction. They
may grow to 2 feet in length and weigh up to 20
pounds.

WHALES

CETACEANS

(to the tune of "Kingdom Coming" or "Year of Jubilo")

"Kingdom Coming" was a million-seller in 1862—it sold 1,000,000 copies of sheet music! The original song was anti-slavery in theme and was popular in both the North and South during the Civil War. Though little remembered today, the song was one of the most popular in its time.

Henry C. Work

Lyrics by Dorry Eldon

These water mammals live in the ocean with the sharks and fish and rays. The six rorquals have throat grooves but not the bow-head, or the right, or gray. The whales are grouped according to their food and how they eat. These have baleen they eat the plankton and those with sharp teeth eat meat.

Chorus

Cetaceans all have lungs, though they live out in the sea These mammals must all rise to the surface for they need the air to breathe.

The whale has two flukes that together make a horizontal tail
It's powerful and it is so muscular it helps propel the whale
The largest of all living animals is the enormous blue
And with the right it has been hunted until now there's just a few
Chorus

Toothed whales include beluga, dolphin, and the sperm and the porpoise too
The orcas are the killer whales that together hunt the ocean blue
Baleen humpbacks leap high from the water and they also sing a song
They sing through their blowholes to other whales as they all swim along
Chorus

WHALES
CETACEANS

Though whales, also called cetaceans, live in the water, they have all the characteristics of mammals: they are warmblooded, give birth to living young, feed their young with milk, and have a backbone. They do not have hair (well, just a few whiskers); instead, they are insulated for warmth with blubber. The name of the order comes from the Greek word meaning "sea monster" and long ago they were considered just that.

The humpback whales, sometimes called " the clowns of the sea," are known for their acrobatic leaps with their long, wing-like flippers.

Whales breathe through nostrils, or **blowholes**, on top of their heads. They also use their blowholes, the area around them, and sometimes their whole heads to create an array of delightful whale noises and songs. They communicate with other whales by these sounds, and the songs of the blue whales can be heard by other whales over 100 miles away! The most notable singers are the humpbacks, who may repeat particular melodies over and over for hours. (Their tapes and CDS are available at most music stores.)

The whale's horizontal tail (a fish tail is vertical) is made up of two flukes. To propel itself through the water, the whale moves its tail up and down, which presses the water backward and pushes the whale forward. The fins and flippers act as rudders for balancing and steering.

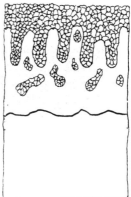
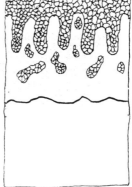

Whales do not have external ears, but they have narrow openings behind their eyes. They have excellent hearing and may even use echolocation to navigate. They send out sounds and listen for the echoes. They know how close their food, a boat, or land is, by the time it takes to hear the echo.

dolphin 12'

orca 20'

Whales are divided into two suborders according to their jaw characteristics and how they eat.

> **1- Baleen whales**: these are the giant "filter feeders" that eat tiny crustaceans and plants collectively called **plankton, zooplankton** or **krill.** They have two blowholes.
> **2- Toothed whales**: these are usually smaller whales (except the sperm whale) that eat fish, squid and octopus. They have one blowhole.

sperm 60'

The whale's skin consists of ridges that hold the outer and inner layers together. Underneath is the blubber, a thick layer of fat (sometimes 2 feet thick) which insulates the whale.

blue 100'
The blue whale is the largest mammal, weighing 100–150 tons!

Pacific gray whale.

BALEEN WHALES

The scientific name for this suborder means "mustached" and refers to the **baleen,** sometimes called **whalebone,** that grows down from the upper jaw like a mustache.

Kingdom : Animal
Phylum: Vertebrata
Class: Mammal
Order: Cetacea
Family: Eschrichtidae
Genus: *Eschrichtius*
Species: *robustus*

Scientific name:
  Eschrichtius robustus
Common name:
  Gray whale

The baleen acts as a sieve as the whale feeds. The whale swims with its mouth open wide and takes in plankton as well as large amounts of water. When the whale closes its jaw, it presses its tongue against the sides of its mouth. This action pushes the seawater out through the baleen but traps the food inside. Baleen whales are also called **filter feeders** because of this filtering process.

The suborder of baleen whales includes only nine species, but they are largest of all mammals.
The **six rorquals** have long, deep grooves on the underside of their throat that expand while feeding. They also have a dorsal fin that can be seen just as they dive. The rorquals are slender, fast swimmers and include the **blue, finback, humpback, sei, Bryde's** and **minke.**

Right whales were considered by whalers to be the "right" whales to hunt. The right swims close to shore, moves slow enough for small boats to chase it, and floats when harpooned.

The baleen is smooth on the outside and frayed on the inside to trap the plankton. The thin strips of baleen were once used in women's corsets.

The **bowheads,** with their large, arching head, were also called "rocknosers" by British whalers because they looked like they were doing headstands when they raised their tails. The bowhead was a popular whale to hunt because its blubber could be half its weight!

The **gray** whale has the longest migration of any mammal: it travels 6,000 miles from the Bering Sea to the warm waters of Baja California where the females have their young.

TOOTHED WHALES

Some of the well-known toothed whale species are the sperm whales, dolphins, porpoises, narwhals, and killer whales, or orcas. These whales often live together in groups called **pods.**

Different species have different kinds and numbers of teeth. Sperm whales have teeth only on the lower jaw and dolphins have up to 300 sharp, spiky teeth. Porpoises have 40 or 50, and male narwhals have only one tooth, a single ivory tusk 8 feet long.

Sperm whales live in the open ocean away from land. This trait protected them from early colonial whaling when only coastal whales were hunted. In the early 1700s, a storm drove a whaling ship out to sea where a sperm whale was caught. From that time on, the sperm became the backbone of the New England whale trade because of the large amount of oil stored in the whale's huge head (one-third of its body). The sperm oil was prized for its quality lighting and lubrication.

Porpoise teeth

Dolphin teeth

Dolphins and Porpoises are the smallest of all whales. Though the names are used interchangeably, there are differences to note.

Several changes happen during the deep dive of the sperm and baleen whales.

Dolphin	**Porpoise**
1- pointed beak nose	**1-** blunt nose, no beak
2- pointed teeth	**2-** spade-shaped teeth
3- sickle-shaped dorsal fin	**3-** triangular dorsal fin
4- sleek body	**4-** smaller, fatter body
5- usually lives in open sea	**5-** usually lives near coast
6- fastest swimmer	

1- A <u>deep</u> breath fills the very inflatable lungs.
2- Blowholes close
3- Heartbeat slows down to one-tenth the normal rate.
4- Blood leaves the surface areas (tail and flippers) to help support vital organs such as the heart and brain.
5- Lungs partially collapse to give oxygen to the blood and muscle cells.
6- The whale blows out water vapor when it returns to the surface.
    Thar she blows!

Narwhals live in the Arctic. Males have a single tusk growing from the left of the upper jaw; females do not have any teeth. Hunters during the Middle Ages provided royal courts of Europe with "unicorn" horns, which were actually the tusk of the narwhal.

Belugas live in large herds in the shore waters of the Arctic coast. They are gray or white and look similar to narwhals, without the tusk. Belugas have 15 to 20 teeth on either jaw to feed on fish, squid and shellfish living in shallow waters. They lack a dorsal fin but are strong, slow swimmers. They squeak and whistle and so are sometimes called "sea canaries."

Orcas, dolphins and porpoises are delightful to watch perform.

Killer whales, or **orcas**, are a species of dolphin. The largest female orcas are about half the size of males, and the males have a very high dorsal fin. They have 40 strong teeth and eat fish, seals, and other small or large whales. They swim and live in family groups called pods.

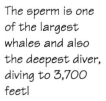

The sperm is one of the largest whales and also the deepest diver, diving to 3,700 feet!

SIRENIANS
SEA COWS, DUGONGS AND MANATEES
(to the tune of "What Shall We do with a Drunken Sailor")

This old sea shanty is based on an Irish dance and march tune that once helped sailors work in rhythm.

Unknown

Lyrics by Dorry Eldon

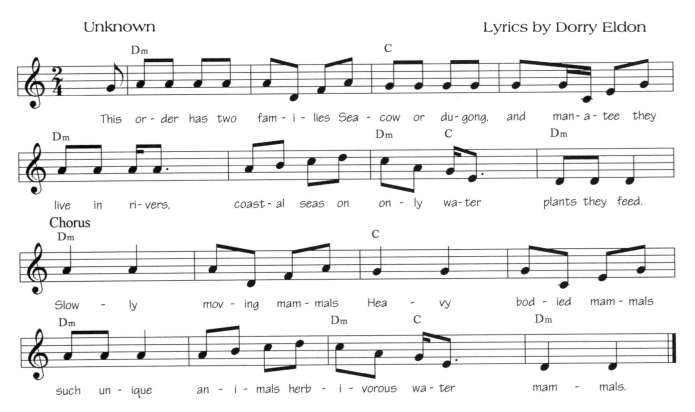

This or-der has two fam-i-lies Sea-cow or du-gong, and man-a-tee they live in ri-vers, coast-al seas on on-ly wa-ter plants they feed.

Chorus

Slow-ly mov-ing mam-mals Hea-vy bod-ied mam-mals such un-ique an-i-mals herb-i-vorous wa-ter mam-mals.

The order is Sirenian
Their bodies, heavy but they swim
With two flippers, but they don't have fins
They may walk the water floor with them
Chorus

Sailors thought they looked like mermaids
So they named them for those sirens
Drawing all to shores nearby them
In salt or fresh water they swim
Chorus

SIRENIANS
SEA COW, DUGONG, MANATEE

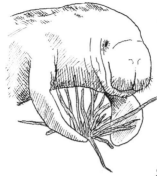

Sirenians have bristles on their noses to help them find their food.

Christopher Columbus reported seeing mammals of this order on one of his voyages to the West Indies. The order's name, sirenian, comes from Columbus' and other sailors' notion that the species resembled mermaids. In Greek, the word for siren means mermaid, and also refers to the sirens of mythology that sang to lure Ulysses and other sailors to their deaths on the islands.

Sirenians are large, herbivorous water-dwelling mammals that eat water plants (not seaweed, which is an algae). They live in tropical seas, coastal rivers and shallow bays where the plants can get the sunlight they need to grow. The order includes two families: the manatee and dugong (including the sea cow, which is now extinct).

All sirenians have bones that are solid and heavy, not hollow, as in other mammals. The heavy bones help the dugong and manatee sink to the bottom to reach their food. They may use their flippers for digging and hunting for food. They also use their flippers for steering, but their large tails propel them through the water.

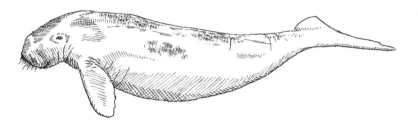

Dugongs and manatees close their eyes, not with eyelids like other mammals, but with a ring of muscles around their eyes. The muscles close around the eye much like the lens of a camera closes around the shutter eye. The ears are located just behind the eyes and are small holes one-fortieth of an inch large. They have sensitive hearing because like other water mammals, they receive sounds through their whole skull, not just through their ears.

Sirenians have nostrils on the tops of their head for easier breathing—they need only to raise the tips out of the water. The manatee's nose points upward, allowing it to easily eat plants and grasses on the

Dugong

Kingdom : Animal
Phylum: Vertebrata
Class: Mammal
Order: Sirenia
Family: Dugongidae
Genus: *Dugong*
Species: *dugon*

Scientific name:
  Dugong dugon
Common name:
  Dugong

water surface. The dugong's nose points down and helps it eat water plants on the ocean floor. Both sirenians can open their nostrils when breathing and shut them when in the water.

Because they shut their nostrils they are not able to smell as people do. Instead, they have a combination smell-taste sense which smells odors in the water. (Land mammals smell odors in the air.) The sirenians have scent glands and rub themselves along rocks or other objects to leave a trail. When other sirenians pass their lips along the same area, they can identify who was there and follow their trail.

Sirenians also have unique horny plates on either side of their lips to help them crush food. The upper lip hangs over the lower and wraps around plants to bring the food to the mouth.

MANATEE

Manatees live in lakes, rivers and lagoons of fresh and marine water. They are the only species that is able to live in both fresh and salt water. Manatees need the warm water to survive and will migrate to warmer areas and gather in temporary herds during cooler winter months. They usually live alone during other seasons of the year, except while rearing their young.

Manatees are larger than any American land mammal and are also the larger of the two kinds of sirenians. They grow to thirteen feet long and weigh up to 3,300 pounds! Manatees include the three following species.

    1- Amazons live in the Amazon River of South America.

    2- West Africans live along the coast of central Africa.

    3- West Indians live along the east and west coasts of Florida.

The Florida manatee mainly eats fresh water plants, but will eat fish when in captivity. American Indians called them "Big Beavers" because their tail is wide, flat, and beaver-like. Not so long ago, manatees were hunted for their meat and old cookbooks include recipes. Their meat is said to taste similar to beef (rather than fish) because both animals eat the same thing—plants.

Manatee

The teeth, which are grinding molars, are formed in the back of the mouth and are pushed forward as the front teeth fall out.

Manatee skin can be two inches thick but is covered with course hairs about one inch apart. These hairs are very sensitive and can sense current changes and directions of moving objects.

Manatee tail

DUGONG, SEA COW

The only surviving member in this genera is the dugong, which weighs up to 1,100 pounds and grows to ten feet. Dugongs live in areas of East Africa, Australia, Indonesia and the Philippines.

A major physical difference between the two sirenian families is the dugong's whale-like notched tail that propels it, sometimes far out in the ocean. Like the manatee, it also uses its flippers for "walking" on the ocean floor as it feeds on water plants. These water plants wear out the dugong's teeth so the back teeth keep growing as they are worn down.

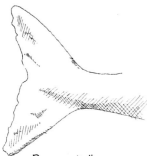

Dugong tail

The Steller sea cow was another species closely related to the dugong. It was the largest of all the sirenians, measuring 26 feet, and was the only sirenian able to live in the cold waters around Bering Island near Alaska. Sea cows were discovered in 1768 during a voyage by Bering himself, and Steller was a famous naturalist aboard that described the huge, defenseless creatures. Shortly afterwards, the sea cows were hunted into extinction for their rich source of blubber.

Manatee and Dugong Differences

The species of these two families may look similar, but major distinguishing characteristics are listed below:

Dugong	Manatee
1- notched tail	**1-** round paddle-shaped tail
2- cleft upper lip	**2-** deeply cleft upper lip
3- males may have tusk-like incisors	**3-** no tusks
4- lives in saltwater, may be ocean going	**4-** lives in salt or fresh water
5- no fingernails on flippers	**5-** fingernails on the end of flippers
6- nose points down	**6-** nose points upward

SINGLE-FAMILY ORDERS
(to the tune of "Should Old Acquaintance be Forgot")

"Auld Lang Syne" is the other name for this well-known Scottish tune. It is
traditionally sung at midnight at the start of a new year.

Unknown   Lyrics by Dorry Eldon

These mam - mals are the or - ders that have on - ly one fam - i -
ly. Com - bin - ing them all in this song fin - ish - es mam - mal stu -
dy. These mam - mals have lit - tle in com - mon this I must re -
peat they're sin - gle fam - ily or - ders that have four legs and four feet.

The elephants have ivory tusks and massive body size.
The trunks make eating easier because they can reach up high
The Asian is one type of two kinds of the elephant
The African has larger ears shaped like that continent

The pangolin is also called the scaly anteater
Protective coated plates help to defend this strange creature
The aardvark is a creature rare it has long ears and snout
It puts it into termite nests and then it pulls them out

The flying lemur looks like a bat but it can't really fly
It leaps from tree to treetop as along the air it glides
The hyraxes look like rodents except for their front teeth
Spaced triangular incisors; and they've sweat pads on their feet

Just recently the elephant shrew; also the tree shrew
Have been reclassified now each has its own order too.
Don't let these mammals be forgot, hold them in your mem'ry
As orders that are special 'cause they have just one family

SINGLE-FAMILY ORDERS
(Elephant, pangolin, aardvark, flying lemur,
hyrax, tree shrew, elephant shrew)

This chapter is really a "catch-all" for the orders that have only one family. Each mammal in this chapter is just too distinct and too unique to be classified in other orders—so scientists have placed each in its own.

ELEPHANT

Elephants are massive. They are the largest land mammals, weighing between 5,000 –14,000 pounds and measuring 6 –12 feet just at the shoulder! Like their size, their appetites are also enormous, and they may spend 18 hours a day eating 500 pounds of bark, leaves and grass![7] A standard rule concerning mammals is: the larger the animal, the more area is needed to support it—and elephants need a lot of room!

Elephants are sometimes called pachyderms, which means "thick-skinned."

A major distinguishing feature, of course, is the elephant's trunk, which may weigh up to 300 pounds! It is actually a long, extended nose with nostrils at the end. It is used not only to breathe through, but also as an upper lip. It makes gathering food easier; from picking up tiny peanuts on the ground, to pulling down leaves from tall trees.

The Asian elephant—
1- Body shape is rounded.
2- Only the male has visible tusks.
3- Dome-shaped forehead.
4- One finger-like structure at the end of the trunk.
5- Five nails on front feet.
6- Has the longest tail that can grow to 5 feet.

Another major feature of the elephants is their tusks, which are really incisor teeth that can grow up to ten feet long! They have other teeth too; their molars erupt one at a time and move forward as the old ones wear down.

The African elephant—
1- Body shape is lean and larger than Asian.
2- Male and female have tusks.
3- Flat forehead.
4- Two finger-like structures at the end of the trunk.
5- Four nails on front feet.

There are two kinds of elephants, the African and Asian, or Indian. The African is the larger of the two, with large ears shaped like the outline of Africa, where it lives. The African elephants are taller and leaner than the rounded Asian; the African have tusks, but only the male Asian have visible tusks.

Other amazing things about elephants:
1- Elephant skin is 1 1/2 inches thick and weighs 2,000 pounds!
2- Elephant ears can be 4 feet wide! [8]

PANGOLIN or SCALY ANTEATER

The name of the order comes from Greek words meaning "wearing scales." The pangolin looks like it is part anteater, reptile and armadillo because of the fingernail-like scales that cover most of its body. The pangolin gets added protection by squirting a smelly liquid and rolling into a ball to protect its face, throat, and belly.

A pangolin looks as though it is walking on its knuckles because its toes curve under to protect its long claws. Its three middle claws can grow up to nine inches long and can easily dig through the plaster-like walls of a termite nest. When it attacks the insect nest it is even protected from biting insects by its extremely thick eyelids and its ability to close its nose and ear openings.

The scales can move sideways in a cutting motion and are even replaced as the old ones wear out.

Pangolins have amazing, long tongues that are connected by muscles to bones way back by the hips. The tongue on the giant pangolin can be two feet long and can reach out one foot from its mouth. It is coated with a sticky substance and slides along insect nest passages picking up thousands of insects— in one night a pangolin may eat 200,000!

Pangolins cannot chew their food because they do not have teeth. The rough walls of part of their stomach have pebbles that work like a chicken's gizzard to help digest their food.

There are seven species of pangolins living in forests, bush or open lands in parts of Africa and Asia. The largest pangolin, the giant, grows to 6 feet and weighs 70 pounds; the smallest, the long-tailed pangolin, is about 3 feet and weighs 4 pounds.

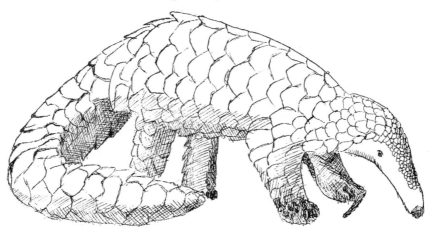

Pangolin

AARDVARK

The aardvark and the pangolin share some similar features but are not closely related. Both have long tongues for eating insects, and powerful claws for digging into insects' nests.

The aardvark lives in open country, bush and forest in Africa. Its name in Afrikaans means "earth pig." It is about 7 feet long from head to end of tail, and weighs up to 140 pounds. Its defenses are its tough skin and its ability to rear up and lash out with its powerful claws. Its digging ability is also a great protection because it can quickly dig a burrow in the hardest of ground.

The aardvark is a solitary, nocturnal mammal with a good sense of smell for locating its food source.

Aardvark also means "ant bear."

Kingdom: Animal
Phylum: Vertebrata
Class: Mammal
Order: Tubulidentata
Family: Orycteropodidae
Genus: *Orycteropus*
Species: *afer*

Scientific name:
  Orycteropus afer
Common name:
  Aardvark

FLYING LEMUR

Flying lemurs, also called colugos, live in Southeast Asia in forest and coconut groves. Their name is a real misnomer because they are not lemurs, nor members of the primate order, nor can they fly. Instead, they make long leaps using the folds of skin (a gliding membrane between their shoulders, arms, ankles and tail) as wings.

Flying lemur

Flying lemurs leap from tree to tree and can "fly" up to 100 feet in one glide! Their gliding membrane does not catch on twigs or branches because it hangs down between their forelegs. Flying lemurs walk upside down and feed on buds, flowers and leaves in this position. They move about in trees with great skill but if they descend to the ground they cannot stand erect!

Adults are about two feet long and weigh three pounds. Their heads look like lemurs' with their large eyes. They have a very unusual lower incisor, a single "comb tooth" with up to twenty comb-like points. (True lemurs also have a similar-looking "comb" but it is composed of individual teeth.) It is thought that the "comb" may strain food, be used as a scraper, or perhaps used for grooming purposes.

HYRAX

Hyraxes, also called dassies, are the size of small rabbits and resemble rodents. But hyraxes have unique features to classify them in their own order. They have a distinctive deep, lower jaw with pointed, triangular upper incisors. There is a large space between the teeth, making them appear as fangs, but true fangs are really long pointed canines—not incisors. The incisors are like rodents': ever-growing and worn down only through use.

Hyraxes are about 18" long. They are sometimes called "little brother of the elephant" because they have flat nails and foot bones that are like those of the elephant.

Hyraxes have sweat glands on the pads of their feet which keep their feet slightly damp. This feature, along with the ability to "cup" their feet, helps them climb on smooth, steep rocks or smooth-barked trees. The sweat glands also produce a scent and are positioned in such a way to leave a scent trail.

All hyraxes have keen hearing, smell and eyesight. They eat plant material but at times may also eat insects. There are three hyrax species and all live in diverse habitats: the forests, lava beds or grasslands in Africa.

Rock hyraxes live on cliffs and ledges in colonies of 5 to 50 animals. **Gray,** or **yellow-spotted** hyraxes also live in rocky areas, and may even share habitat with rock hyraxes. Gray hyraxes, however, live together in colonies of up to one hundred hyraxes. **Tree,** or **bush**, hyraxes are arboreal and live solitary lives, or they may live in small groups of two or three. They make a distinctive call at night in a series of croaks that ends in a loud scream.

ELEPHANT SHREW

Until recently the elephant shrews were classified with other shrews in the insectivore order. General agreement has been reached just recently to classify these unique species in their own order.

The elephant shrew has a long, narrow snout, as its name suggests. It is also flexible like the elephant's and can move in a circular manner. Its nostrils are also located at the end of the snout.

Elephant shrews live in Africa and Zanzibar.

Elephant shrews live in rocky areas, forests, and grassy plains. Because their feet are not really made for digging, they often reside in old rodent burrows, live hidden in brush, or a make shallow, cup-like nest.

Most of these little animals live alone or in pairs, but one species lives in small colonies. Most young are born covered with hair, able to see and able to walk. Adult elephant shrews usually move on all fours, but hop or leap when frightened.

TREE SHREW

The tree shrew, like the elephant shrew, has been difficult to classify. Until as recently as 1983 these mammals were classified with primates based on similarities of particular arteries and size of braincase. They also have the long snout of shrews in the order of insectivores, but are distinct enough to be classified as a separate order.

The tree shrew is not a kind of shrew.

The order's scientific name comes from the word "squirrel" in Malay. Tree shrews look and move like squirrels, with their quick running and tree-climbing abilities, as they scurry for fruit and insects (squirrels do not eat insects). Like squirrels, they also have keen senses of smell, hearing and vision. A main outward physical difference between these two animals is their long, whiskerless snouts.

Tree shrews live in Malaysia, Asia and the Philippines. Though some species are terrestrial, most are arboreal, living in trees. A mating pair has a strong bond and will build a nest for the young and a separate nest for themselves. When the young are just over a month old, they join their parents' nest.

Some species of tree shrews are omnivores and also eat mice and lizards.

ECOLOGY

(to the tune of "Sweet Betsy From Pike")

"Sweet Betsy From Pike" was one of the most popular songs in California in the 1850s during the gold rush. It was written by John A. Stone, one-time prospector turned minstrel, who published it in his popular songbook: *Put's Original California Songster*. The melody is from an old English song: "Villikins and His Dinah."

Unknown   Lyrics by Doug Eldon

E - col - o - gy is sci - en - ti - fic stu - dy of re - la - tion - ships and in - ter - ac - tions, you see, of liv - ing things one with an - oth - er as well as with their en - vi - ron - ment, where they all dwell. Sing - ing e - col - o - gy col - o - gy col - o - gy

The living and nonliving environment
Are factors which are all interdependent
A community is all the organisms
That live together in an ecosystem
Singing ecolo-gy colo-gy cology

A group of the same kind of living thing
In the same area is the population
The number that's found of that single species
Is known as the population density
Singing ecolo-gy colo-gy cology

A habitat is a place where it is good
For a living thing to find its shelter and food
But the way that it lives and the things that it does
Creates the particular niche that it has
Singing ecolo-gy cology cology

Relationships include competition
The struggle with others in ecosystems
And with the environment to stay alive
Competing for the basic needs to survive
Singing ecolo-gy colo-gy cology

Predation is predators killing what they
Will then consume which is known as their prey
This relationship doesn't just benefit one
For predators help control populations
Singing ecolo-gy colo-gy cology

Living together is symbiosis
Where one or more organisms benefit
Commensal helps one, mutual helps them both
Parasites benefit at expense of their hosts
Singing ecolo-gy colo-gy cology

ECOLOGY

Ecology is the study of the relationships and interactions of living things with each other and with their environment. The word ecology comes from the Greek words meaning "house" and "the study of."

An animal's home is called a **habitat**—a particular place where it finds food, shelter, and whatever else it may need. A forest may be a deer's habitat, but that deer may be a habitat for a deer tick. An ocean may be a whale's habitat, but the whale may be a habitat for a barnacle.

A deer is a habitat for a tick.

The **environment** is all living and nonliving things in a particular area. These two things are called **environmental factors**:
> **1- biotic factors**, which are living plants, animals, fungi, protists and monerans.
> **2- abiotic factors** which are non-living things such as water, air, light, soil and climate.

In any particular place, the factors in an environment **interact**, or have an effect upon each other. These factors are also **interdependent,** which means they depend upon each other. For example, the climate of an area determines what plants grow there, which in turn determines what animals live in that area, either eating those plants or eating other animals.

All the factors are interconnected in some way with other factors around them. This whole system of interacting living and nonliving factors in an environment is called an **ecosystem**. An ecosystem may be as large as an ocean or as small as a drop of pond water.

A coniferous forest can be:
an ecosystem,
a community
and a habitat

A **community** is all of the <u>living</u> organisms interacting in an ecosystem. A coniferous forest community may include plants such as conifer trees, ferns, lichens and mosses; mushrooms and other fungi; and animals such as mice, squirrels, other rodents, song birds, owls, deer, bobcats, and humans. In this community all of these living things are biotic factors in a coniferous forest ecosystem.

A **population** refers to all of one kind of organism in one area. For example, in the forest community, if all of the deer were being considered, they would be the deer population. The **population density** is the number of that one species in a certain size area. An example could be twenty deer per square mile.

All the different **populations** *of an area make up a* **community.**

All **communities** *plus* **abiotic factors** *make up an* **ecosystem.**

ECOSYSTEM RELATIONSHIPS

The way that an organism fits into an ecosystem is called its **niche**. A niche is also the part that the organism plays in the community. Consider owls and mice:

    1- the owl's niche in a forest community may be eating mice, which keeps the mouse population from getting too large.

    2- the mouse's niche includes eating certain seeds, and providing food for owls.

In every ecosystem or community there is a limited amount of food, space, water, or other basic need. An organism that is trying to satisfy its needs must **compete** against other organisms in the same area which need the same things.

The struggle for survival is also with "**the elements**"—the abiotic or nonliving factors in the environment. These elements may include such things as weather conditions, water, or light. In general, the organisms best able to compete are the ones that survive. This concept is what is called the "**survival of the fittest**"; or the survival of those most able to compete.

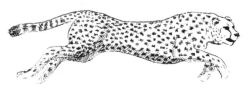

Any animal that feeds on other animals is called a **predator.** The animal that gets eaten is known as the **prey**, and the act of being hunted is called **predation**. Predators are important for population control of many species, such as rodents.

The word **symbiosis** means "together-life," and refers to particular types of relationships between two organisms. There are three forms of symbiosis or symbiotic relationships:

    1- commensal: one benefits while the other is neither harmed nor helped. Example: remoras and sharks.

    2- mutual: both benefit. Examples: ants getting, honeydew from aphids, while protecting them; myna birds on rhinos; lichen (alga and fungus).

    3- parasitic: one benefits while the other is harmed. Example: heart worms in a dog.

    A **parasitoid** is a parasite that actually causes the host animal to die. Example: wasp larvae that feed on caterpillars, killing them.

ECOLOGY PART 2

(to the tune of "The Campbells are Coming")

This melody is an old Scottish jig.

Unknown   Lyrics by Doug Eldon

Plants make the food and they are pro-du-cers an-i-mals that eat them are con-sum-ers

eat-ers of dead things are scav-en-gers bac-teri-a and fun-gi are de-com-pos-ers.

Chorus

E-col-o-gic-ly the en-er-gy flows round and a-gain the cy-cle goes

from the sun to au-to-trophs to in-ter-de-pen-dent het-er-o-trophs.

The plant-eaters are the herbivores
The meat-eaters are the carnivores
If they eat both then they're omnivores
And that is what you and I are, of course
Chorus

Falling water is precipitation
Liquid to gas is evaporation
Which from a plant leaf is transpiration
And turning back to clouds is condensation
Chorus

There's cycles involving nitrogen
Carbon dioxide and oxygen
Loose in the atmosphere and then
In soil, plants, animals and back again
Chorus

ENERGY FLOWS

There are three kinds of living things:
1- PRODUCERS (plants)

2- CONSUMERS
(eat plants or animals)
1- herbivores

2- carnivores

3- scavengers

4- omnivores

3- DECOMPOSERS
(break down dead plants and animals)

FOOD CHAIN

Food chains, food webs, and **energy cycles** are all terms to describe the transfer of energy from the sun to plants; and then to animals and other organisms.

Plants are called **producers**, or even "food factories," because they actually make food. Because plants can make their own food, instead of having to eat, they are given the term **autotroph**, which means "self-feeder." The way in which they produce their food is a process called **photosynthesis**.

Using the light energy from the sun, plants make simple sugars out of air and water. Light energy is changed into chemical energy, which can then be stored in the sugar molecules. These molecules are made up of the elements carbon, oxygen, and hydrogen, and are therefore called **carbohydrates**.

When the plant needs energy, as for growth, it uses the stored chemical energy by "burning" (breaking apart) the carbohydrate molecules in a process called **respiration**.

The energy from the sun is made available to animals only after plants change the light energy to chemical energy. A **consumer** is an animal that eats plants or plant-eating animals. As presented throughout the mammal chapters, there are four types of consumers:

> **1- herbivores** (plant-eaters) are called primary consumers. Examples: deer, rabbit, mouse.
> **2- carnivores** (meat- or flesh-eaters) are called secondary consumers. Examples: cat, dog.
> **3- scavengers** (dead animal-eaters) eat dead things. Examples: vulture, buzzard, hyena.
> **4- omnivores** (anything-eaters) eat plants and animals. Examples: opossum, human.

Besides producers and consumers, there is a third kind of living thing; it gets its energy not by eating, but by breaking down dead plants and animals. These are the **decomposers**. Fungi and bacteria are the most important decomposers. Without them, dead organisms would not rot or decompose, but would just pile up!

Because consumers and decomposers cannot make their own food, but have to eat to get energy, they are given the term **heterotroph**, meaning "other-eater."

Feeding habits:
  Autotrophs (self-feeders)
   -producers are plants
  Heterotrophs (other-eaters)
   -consumers and
    decomposers

As seen on the previous page, a **food chain** shows how energy is used and transferred from one organism to another. Stated more simply, a food chain is how one organism is eaten by another organism.

A **food web** contains many food chains and shows how they are all interdependent, or connected. They can be very complicated!

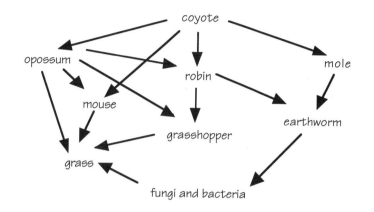

ENERGY CYCLES

Food chains and food webs explain how the sun's energy is transferred throughout the ecosystem, from light, to plants, to animals, to decomposers. There are many other nonliving elements that flow or cycle throughout ecosystems. Some of the more common cycles are:

> **1- Water**
> **2- Nitrogen**
> **3- Carbon dioxide**
> **4- Oxygen**

THE WATER CYCLE

The water cycle involves:

> **1- evaporation** from the earth's surface
> **2- transpiration** from plants
> **3- condensation** into clouds
> **4- precipitation** back to the ground

1- Evaporation. Heat energy from the sun causes water to **evaporate**, or change from liquid to a gas called **water vapor**. In this way water and heat are removed from the ocean, the ground, or from some other surface that had liquid water on it. As a gas, the water vapor has absorbed heat energy, and therefore is usually warmer and less dense than the air around it. This makes water vapor rise, because it is lighter than the air.

Evaporation

Transpiration

2- Transpiration. When water evaporates from a leaf, it is called **transpiration**. Water is absorbed through the plant's roots and drawn up through the plant. This continually moving flow of water from the soil to all the plant cells does several things:

1- keeps the stems, leaves, and flowers erect.
2- supplies the leaves with water needed in photosynthesis.
3- draws minerals (nitrogen, potassium, etc.) from the soil to the different plant parts.
4- cools the plant as the heat is removed through the process of evaporation.

When the water gets to tiny holes on the leaf's surface, it is exposed to air and evaporates. In so doing, the evaporating water molecule draws other water molecules up to take its place. This whole process of transpiration moves tons of water from the soil, up through the plant—against the pull of gravity—and finally into the air.

Condensation

3- Condensation. As it rises, however, water vapor cools until it gets to a certain temperature called the **dew point**. At that temperature the water vapor becomes dense again. It **condenses** back into liquid water, becoming clouds. When that happens, the heat that was keeping the water as vapor is released into the atmosphere, making the air warmer up high. The water and the heat energy that had been at ground level have been transferred to higher altitudes. This is the first half of the water cycle.

Precipitation includes:
- rain
- hail (rain frozen while in the cloud)
- sleet (rain frozen while falling)
- snow (water frozen into ice crystals while in clouds)

4- Precipitation. Eventually, the droplets of water that had condensed into clouds combine to form larger droplets. These droplets continue to grow, and when they are heavy enough, fall back to the ground as **precipitation**.

Once on the ground, the liquid water flows downhill in rivers and streams, or underground in aquifers. The water may get absorbed by plants along the way, but much of it ends up in bodies of water such as lakes or oceans. Either way, the cycle then begins again with liquid water evaporating.

NITROGEN CYCLE

Nitrogen is an element used in the production of protein. It is especially important for plants because it is needed for making chlorophyll, necessary for photosynthesis. When plants are supplied with enough nitrogen, they will more likely be green and healthy; when they are not, they will often be yellowish and weak. Nitrogen is therefore one of the most important elements in plant fertilizers. (Check it out next time you go to the plant nursery!)

Although nitrogen makes up about 78 percent of the air we breathe, it is not in a form that plants or animals can use. The nitrogen that is "free" in the atmosphere needs to be "fixed" into combinations with oxygen, forming compounds called nitrates.

The nitrogen that is fixed into the soil by bacteria, or added as nitrogen fertilizer, is first used by plants. When these plants are eaten, the nitrogen compounds are used by animals, then pass back to the soil in the animal wastes or when the animals die. The nitrogen may pass from soil to plant to animal and back to soil, but this is not the complete nitrogen cycle.

The nitrogen that is fixed into nitrates or other nitrogen compounds is freed into the atmosphere in one way: by another kind of bacteria—**denitrifying bacteria**. In this way the nitrogen cycle is made complete.

> The process of nitrogen fixation is done in three main ways:
>
> 1- by certain nitrogen-fixing bacteria living in the soil, feeding on dead or decaying matter, or growing on roots of plants called **legumes**, such as peas, beans and clover
>
> 2- by blue-green algae living in water—the first link in the ocean food chains
>
> 3- by factories that make fertilizer

CARBON AND OXYGEN CYCLES

These two cycles are often discussed together, because they are interrelated. The small amount of carbon dioxide in the atmosphere, less than one percent, makes carbon available to plants. In the process of photosynthesis, carbon becomes part of simple sugars, or carbohydrates. Oxygen from the dioxide is released into the air as a by-product.

Oxygen makes up about 20 percent of the atmosphere. It is breathed and used by plants and animals in the process of respiration, which involves breaking down carbohydrates. Carbon dioxide is given off as a by-product of respiration, completing the cycle.

> For purposes of understanding, the energy cycles have been simplified because they can become very complicated! Other cycles include:
>   phosphorus
>   sulfur
>   potassium

BIOMES

(to the tune of "Get Along Little Dogies" or "Whoopy Ti Yi Yo")

The melody is an Irish one that is still heard in that country, though of course, sung with different words. Somehow the tune made it to the Old American West where it was used as a day-herding call by the drivers of longhorns on their trails.

Unknown

Lyrics By Doug Eldon

Des - erts are dry but the tem - pera-ture va - ries tun - dras are
dry, but all year it may freeze grass - lands get more rain and
may be called prai - ries sa - van - nas are grass-lands that al - so have
trees. Oh the bi - omes are re - gions with sim - i - lar cli - mate
(pre - ci - pi - ta - tion and tem - pera - tures) the cli - mate de - ter-mines soil
and veg - e - ta - tion which then de - ter-mines the kinds of crea - tures

In coniferous forests there are conifer trees
Needleleaf evergreens like pine and fir
Deciduous forests have trees that drop broad leaves
Rainforests are wet and warm most of the year
Chorus

The freshwater biome includes streams and rivers
Lakes, ponds, swamps, marshes, and lands that are wet
The saltwater biome, the seas and the oceans
Called the marine it's too large to forget
Chorus

BIOMES

Scientists have long observed that even on different continents, particular plants and animals live in specific regions or areas. They have developed different ways of classifying these regions based on similarities in location, climate, plants and animals. These regions are called **biomes**.

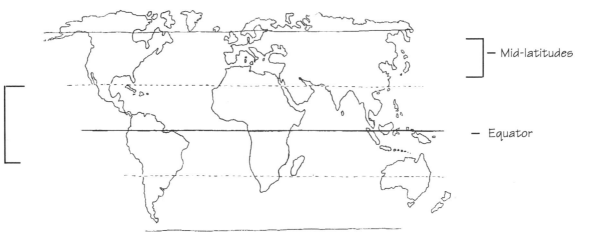

A soil profile is a long, narrow sample showing different soil layers. Soil is formed from rock, sand, silt, clay and dead plant and animal matter.

Climate is weather over a long period of time, especially yearly precipitation (rain, snow, etc.) and average temperatures. Climate is one of the main factors that determine the **vegetation**—the plants that grow in a particular area. Climate is determined by:

    1- latitude (distance north or south of the equator)
    2- altitude (the elevation above sea level)
    3- location on a continent or near a body of water

The vegetation determines what animals live in a particular area. Many large plant-eaters, such as the hoofed mammals, live in grasslands. These herbivores provide food for large predators such as lions and tigers. Neither of these large animals are found in the desert where plants are scarce.

Vegetation is of major importance. Plants are consumable and renewable resources—we can use them and we can replant them for food, building materials (for shelter), fuel, and fiber (for clothing). The plants that grow naturally without being planted or cared for by humans are called **natural vegetation**. Any plant grown with the help of humans is considered an **agricultural** or **horticultural crop**.

Six land biomes (from the driest to the wettest):
   desert
   tundra
   grassland
    (and savanna)
   coniferous forest
   deciduous forest
   tropical rainforest
Two water biomes:
   fresh water
   marine

DESERT

A desert is a dry or **arid** land where total precipitation is less than ten inches. The lack of moisture is what characterizes a desert, not high temperatures! A desert may be hot-dry, such as the Sonoran Desert of the southwestern United States, or cool-dry, such as in eastern Oregon.

The largest desert in the world, the Sahara Desert of northern Africa, is mostly shifting sand dunes with few, if any, plants. The driest desert, the Atacama of central Chile, which gets absolutely no measurable rainfall, has no natural vegetation.

The vegetation of most deserts is rather sparse and provides little ground cover, making deserts rather barren, exposed to sun and wind. Most desert plants have shallow roots that are spread out to absorb rainwater quickly. Many desert plants also have deep taproots to reach down to groundwater. Others such as cacti and succulents store water in their fleshy stems.

The animals that live in the desert are usually nocturnal, coming out of burrows to feed at night. They are able to live without much water, getting what they need from the food they eat. There are many animals that are well suited for the desert which often fulfill important environmental roles. For example, the nectar-eating bats pollinate saguaro cacti while they feed.

Desert animals include:
  scorpion
  rattlesnake
  tortoise
  roadrunner
  kangaroo rat
  coyote

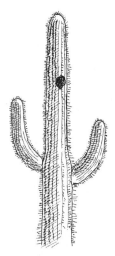

Desert plants include:
  cacti
  hard grasses
  seasonal flowers
  woody shrubs

TUNDRA

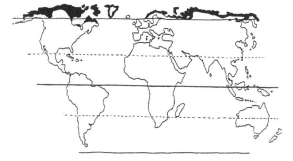

The tundra is basically a cold desert found near the North and South Poles. There is less than 12 inches of precipitation, mostly snow, but the temperatures are below freezing for most of the year. What results is **permafrost**—soil that is permanently frozen below about 3 inches. An **arctic fell field** may also result from rocks being shattered by intense freezing.

A **polar biome** is sometimes distinguished from tundra. This cold but dry biome surrounds both the North and South poles and occurs at the tops of tall mountains.

Alpine tundra occurs at high elevations, above the **timberline** (the area where trees stop growing) but below the zone of barren rock and permanent snow on mountain tops. The biggest difference between alpine tundra and arctic tundra is the amount of direct sunshine warming alpine tundra in lower latitudes, which prevents the formation of permafrost.

Tundra animals:
 lemmings
 reindeer
 caribou
 walrus
 polar bear

The only plants that can grow on the exposed rocky surfaces or small patches of soil are mosses, lichens, and a few small shrubs such as the dwarf willow.

Animals able to live in this cold, dry climate include herbivores that feed on the few tundra plants, and carnivores that feed on herbivores.

Tundra plants include:
 moss
 lichen
 dwarf willow

GRASSLANDS

Grasslands cover about one-fourth of all the land surface of the earth and exist on every continent except Antarctica. They are usually near the center of the continent, but their temperatures vary greatly from hot all year round to very cold in the winter. All receive from 10 to 20 inches of precipitation, which determine the kind and height of grasses. Semidesert grasslands support mostly short, annual grasses called **hard grasses**; grassy tundra in high latitudes and high elevations supports short **perennial grasses**.

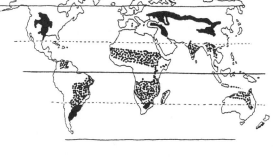

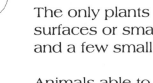

short grass

■ Grasslands
▨ Savannas

Grasslands are given different names on different continents—**prairie** in central United States and Canada; **steppes** (pronounced "steps") in Asia; **pampas** in South America; and **veldt** in Africa.

The grasslands in North America are divided into three regions based on the height of the grasses:

> **1- shortgrass prairie** in the arid western part of the Great Plains; grasses grow from 6 inches to 2 feet.
> **2- mixed-height prairie** in the mid-western Great Plains has short, medium, and tall grasses.
> **3- tallgrass prairie** in the wetter eastern region is where native grass species grow to 12 feet tall!

medium grass

tallgrass

Grasses are in a family of plants with narrow leaves called **blades**, flowers that are pollinated by wind and so are not showy or colorful, and root systems that are **fibrous**—many filaments spreading throughout the soil. There are **annual** grasses which re-seed themselves each year, but most grasses are **perennial**, resprouting from the same root crown.

Because grasslands receive little precipitation, the roots must be able to absorb ground moisture effectively. The fibrous root system of grasses is very effective. If all the roots of a perennial ryegrass plant were lined up, they would stretch almost 400 miles!

People have depended on the seeds from grass plants for thousands of years. The most important part of agriculture has always been the growing of what are called **cereal** or **grain crops**—including wheat, rice, oats, barley, and rye. Other grasses have fed livestock—cattle, sheep, and horses—and have provided food and habitat for wild animals.

Grassland plants include:
   grass (obviouslyl)
   forbs (annual flowers)

Grassland animals include:
   grasshoppers
   prairie dogs
   antelopes
   bison
   elephants
   giraffes
   kangaroos
   coyote

Sugar comes from a tall tropical grass, sugarcane, and corn (also called **maize**) is a tall grass native to the Americas that has fed people and livestock.

SAVANNAS

Savannas are simply grasslands with trees, either singly or in small clusters, but total precipitation in savannas is higher than in grasslands. A good example of a true savanna stretches across Africa, where acacia and baobab trees are scattered in the grasslands. In addition to grass and trees, savannas may include shrubs.

Savannas have grasses and forbs, but also have scattered trees and shrubs.

There are other kinds of grasslands and savannas that do not include grass:
    1- the **savanna woodland**, also called **parkland**, such as in the western United States where yellow pine, or pinyon pine and juniper grow in open stands.
    2- the **thornbush** or **thorn forest**, and **tropical scrub**, in which tall, thorny, woody shrubs grow close together.
    3- the **semidesert** in the western United States features sagebrush that has taken over grass lands that had been overgrazed.
    4- **heath** is mostly heather and mosses, and is found at higher elevations or cooler climates; called **moors** in the British Isles.

CONIFEROUS FORESTS

Coniferous forests consist of evergreen trees called **conifers** that have these characteristics:

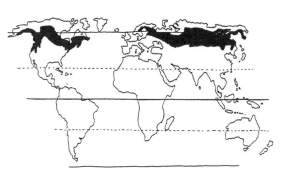

1- conical shape with straight trunks.
2- seeds that come in cones.
3- needlelike leaves that stay green all year.

The shape of the trees and the relatively short branches enable the conifers to withstand the winter snow and wind. The waxy coating on the small, narrow needles prevents the leaves from freezing.

The trees shade the ground too much for lower layers of vegetation. The cold winters, as well as short and cool summers, do not permit bacteria to decompose leaves that do fall to the ground. The result is soil that is usually poor. This infertile soil limits the types of plants; most coniferous forests have only a few species of trees.

Coniferous forest animals include:
 beetle
 squirrel
 owl
 deer
 moose
 wolf

There are several types of coniferous forests, depending on the amount of precipitation, temperature and elevation:

1- temperate rainforest in the mildly cool and very wet climate of the Pacific Northwest.
2- muskeg is a bog or swamp-forest caused by poor drainage.
3- taiga is a cold, woodland savanna found just below the treeless tundra.

Coniferous forest plants include:
 Douglas fir
 pine
 hemlock
 cedar
 redwood
 fern

DECIDUOUS FORESTS

Deciduous trees are tall, broadleaf trees that grow where summers are warm and wet, and winters are cold and wet. Forests of these trees are also called **summergreen deciduous** because the leaves grow in the spring, remain all summer, and fall off in autumn.

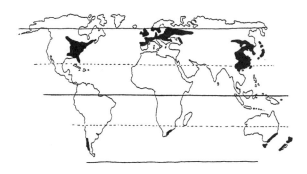

The coniferous forest is always dark from the ever-present shade, but the deciduous forest is light in spring before the leaves grow. The result is a greater diversity of plants and animals living in deciduous forests than in coniferous forests.

Deciduous forest
animals include:
  spider
  millipede
  snail
  salamander
  mouse
  squirrel
  raccoon
  deer

Similar species of mammals live in both forests, but more invertebrates and amphibians are able to live in the deciduous forest. This is because of the climate and the several layers of vegetation in deciduous forests:

> **1-** the tree **canopy**, or upper layer, is made up of the dominant species, such as oak and maple.
> **2-** the **understory**, which is layers of shorter trees and shrubs.
> **3-** the **herb layer** of wildflowers, ferns, and grasses that grow mainly in spring before the leaves in the canopy shade the ground.
> **4-** the **ground layer** of mosses and fungi that grows where the decomposing leaf litter produces a **humus**, or rich, fertile soil. With the warmer temperatures, bacteria is active in decomposing the fallen leaves, returning nutrients to the soil.

Deciduous forest
plants include:
  oak
  maple
  hickory
  ash
  sycamore
  beech
  cottonwood
  elm

There are variations and mixtures of both deciduous and coniferous forests: **Evergreen-hardwood** forests of oaks and pine grow in climates with hot, dry summers and mild, wet winters; a **chaparral** is a "dwarf forest" of scrub and evergreen hardwoods.

RAINFORESTS

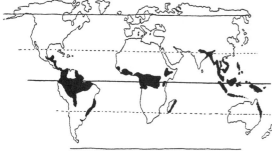

The term **rainforest** refers to a forest where the rainfall is usually greater than 80 inches per year. True **tropical rainforests** are generally close to the equator— and may be called equatorial rainforests— and have a long wet season and a short dry season.

If they are on a mountainside rainforests are called **montane rainforests**; if they are usually enveloped in clouds they are **cloud forests**.

Rainforests that are farther from the equator are seasonal, and receive their rain from heavy summer rains called **monsoons**. Many of the trees in these **monsoon** or **wet-dry forests** are deciduous. Other names for these forests are **tropical deciduous forests**, or **tropical moist forests**. Because of their dry season, these tropical rainforests have fewer species of trees, plants, and animals than equatorial rainforests.

Some cooler rainforests exist along the North Pacific coast and along the southeastern coast of the United States.

Goliath beetle

The animals that live in rainforests include some of the most unusual. The ecosystems in the canopy itself are complex, with interrelationships and interdependencies that have yet to be understood.

Rainforest animals include many kinds of primates, felines, birds, bats, and especially invertebrates such as insects. Over 40 species of ants were found to live in one tree, and the colors and variety of butterflies attract collectors from the world over.

Tropical rainforests receive the most annual rainfall, up to 400 inches (33 feet!), and have little or no dry season. Equatorial rainforests have more kinds of trees, plants, animals, and fungi than any other biome. More than half of all the species of living things in the world live in these rainforests! The diversity of life, called **biodiversity**, is the greatest here where the growing conditions for plants are the best. In these rainforests there is a constant supply of rainfall, consistently warm temperatures, and direct and intense sunlight all year.

The trees that grow in equatorial rainforests all have broad leaves that they do not drop, which is why these forests are called **broadleaf evergreen forests**. The trees are tall and grow close together, forming a continuous canopy of foliage. There may be two or three layers of the canopy: a few taller trees emerging above the rest, called **emergent trees**, and an understory of small, slender trees with narrow crowns growing to perhaps half the height of the rest.

Thick woody vines called **lianas** climb up the tree trunks and into the branches of the canopy. These may be slender ropes such as Tarzan would use, or they may be massive vines up to eight inches in diameter!

Plants such as ferns, orchids, mosses, and lichens use trees and lianas for support, sometimes covering trunks, branches, and foliage. These are given the name **epiphyte**, which means "plant growing upon another plant."

A **jungle** is a dense, tangled growth of thickly branching shrubs, bamboos, lianas, and other plants. This kind of growth is possible only where sunlight reaches the forest floor—along rivers or at other edges of the forest, or where the original forest has been logged or burned.

The **forest floor** of equatorial rainforests is typically quite open, cooler, and darker than the canopy. Very few plants can grow below the canopy because it is so dense that little light can penetrate.

The warm temperatures and abundant moisture are ideal for bacteria and fungi to quickly decompose any plant or animal matter that falls to the forest floor. Most nutrients are quickly absorbed by the shallow roots of forest plants, with the help of fungi that grow on the roots, called **mycorrhizae**.

Layers of rainforest showing emergent trees, canopy, understory and forest floor.

A strangler fig begins growing, up in a tree. It gradually grows down and around the trunk, strangling the host tree.

FRESHWATER BIOME

The freshwater biome includes running water and still water. The freshwater biome affects and is affected by the climate, soil, vegetation and animals of the surrounding region.

The area surrounding running water such as rivers and streams is called the **riparian** zone. This zone should be (but is not) included in this biome because it is very much affected by the water. It may be a narrow or wide area depending on how far the effects of the water reach. The trees and shrubs that thrive in the moist soil of the riparian zone affect the water in several ways:

1- They provide shade that keeps the water from becoming heated by the sun, which would affect the aquatic plants and animals.
2- They keep the banks from quickly eroding, which would cause muddying of the water and filling in of the streambed with silt, both of which would affect the animal life.
3- They provide habitats—food and shelter— for mammals and other animals that cannot live in the water at all times.

The freshwater biome includes running water, such as streams and rivers mentioned above, but it also in-cludes several still-water **wetland** ecosystems:

1- seasonal wetlands are wet for part of the year but dry for a season; the plants and animals must endure both conditions
2- bogs may be flooded or saturated soil with thick layers of mosses that partially decompose into what is called **peat**
3- marshes are usually shallow, still water overgrown with grasses, rushes, or reeds
4- swamps are shallow, still water overgrown with trees; **muskegs** are in old lake basins
5- ponds are still bodies of water smaller than lakes that may have floating plants
6- lakes are larger than ponds

Several or all of these freshwater ecosystems may be joined together, but each has its special conditions, or **factors**, that make it a suitable habitat for particular organisms. Factors include:

1- the speed at which the water moves.
2- the amount of oxygen and food in or near the water.
3- the temperature of the water, air, or soil.
4- the amount and intensity of sunlight.

Spirogyra
(green algae)

Plants that live in or near fresh water include:
algae
duckweed
elodea
cattail rush
sedge
waterlily
mangrove

Animals that live in or near still or running fresh water include:
water flea
mayfly
dragonfly
crayfish
snapping turtle
salamander
frog
trout
kingfisher
duck
beaver
river otter
osprey

Mangrove trees grow in swamps. The difference between a swamp and a marsh is not always clear, especially because the two terms have been used for the same conditions.

MARINE BIOME

The last biome is also the largest, covering over 70 percent of the earth! The marine biome is also the most diverse, the most complex, and the most important: it affects all the other biomes because it determines the climate of a region.

One characteristic of this biome makes it different from all others—the salt in the water. Seawater contains 3.5% salt, which only sea plants and animals are able to tolerate.

The marine biome is divided into three zones:
1- The **open ocean** has an upper lever that sunlight reaches, and a dark level where light does not reach. The greatest amount of marine life live in the "light" zone, especially in the shallow waters over the **continental shelves**, the area near continents. Here, free-floating algae, protozoa, and small invertebrates called plankton, get the light they need, and minerals that are brought from deeper water by currents.

2- The **intertidal** zone is along the shore. Here the rising and falling tide means that the plants and animals must be able to endure exposure to air and the crashing of waves. Tidepools, reefs, rocks, and even sandy beaches are habitats for many kinds of invertebrates, fishes, birds, and marine mammals.

3- Estuaries are a third major zone in the marine biome. Here the water is **brackish**—a mixture of fresh and salt water. The bays, mud flats, and salt marshes that are included in this zone are exposed to variations in temperature and **salinity** (saltiness). Mineral nutrients are deposited by streams and rivers that flow into estuaries, creating very unique habitats. Many kinds of plants, invertebrates, and birds found in estuaries, are found in no other area in the world.

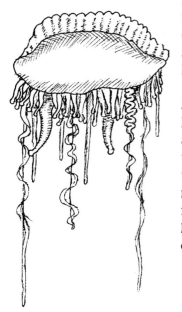

Animals of the marine biome include the dangerous Portuguese man o' war.

An intertidal zone.

Plants of the marine biome include kelp, a type of algae.

APPENDIX

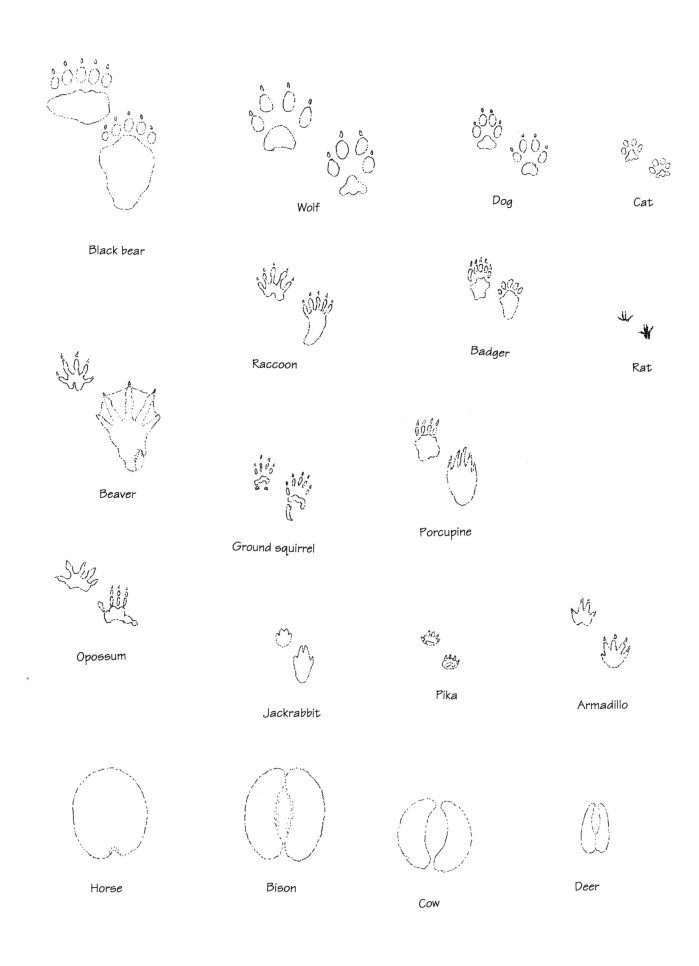

Black bear

Wolf

Dog

Cat

Raccoon

Badger

Rat

Beaver

Ground squirrel

Porcupine

Opossum

Jackrabbit

Pika

Armadillo

Horse

Bison

Cow

Deer

MAMMALS

(to the tune of "Marine's Hymn")
"From the halls of Montezuma, to the shores of Tripoli..."
By Doug and Dorry Eldon 1995

There are different kinds of mammals but they all have hair or fir
And the babies all get to drink milk that they get from their mother
Monotremes lay eggs instead of giving birth to young alive
And the immature marsupials crawl to pouches to survive

There are nineteen orders of placental mammals in this class
You can learn of them in other songs but they're listed here real fast
They are grouped by how and what they eat, how they move or their features
Or where and how they live help to classify diverse creatures

There are rodents and the rodent-like, insect-eaters and flying bats
Carnivores and those without real teeth and the trunk-nosed elephants
There are many kinds with hoofs and there are water dwellers too
Primates you will remember for the order includes you

Mammals that walk and live on the land are all terrestrial
And the kinds that live up in the trees are all arboreal
Mammals that live in saltwater seas are what we call marine
There are also those that fly so high or can glide from tree to tree

MONOTREMES and MARSUPIALS

(to the tune of "Aura Lea")
By Dorry Eldon 1995

Koala, wombat, kangaroo and the wallaby
They are pouched marsupials there's sixteen families.

Chorus:
Monotremes, marsupials most live in Australia
But the opossums have a pouch, and live in America

The young is born quite immature, it crawls to the pouch
It develops there within, before it comes out
Chorus

Many are herbivores, others carnivores
There's also insectivores, opposums are omnivores
Chorus

The two egg-laying monotremes live near Australia
There's the duck-billed platypus and the echidna
Chorus

CARNIVORES and PINNIPEDS

(to the tune of "She'll Be Coming Round the Mountain")
by Dorry and Doug Eldon 1995

Oh there are flesh eating mammals that are known
As the carnivores throughout the world they roam
Chasing mammals for their meat
It is what they need to eat
These are mammals that as carnivores are known

They can smell their food with noses that are long
And their legs are rather muscular and strong
They have claws upon their feet
Helps them hold on to their meat
And their lower jaw is hinged to move so free

Oh the carnivores have specialized back teeth
Carnassials they use for shearing meat
The four canine teeth are pairing
Pointed teeth they use for tearing
Their premolars are for cutting what they eat

In the order there are seven families
Weasels, mongoose and raccoon are three of these
Foxes, wolves, and dogs are canines
All the cats are known as felines
And the others are the bears and the hy—e—nas

Pinnipeds are the aquatic carnivores
And they live out in the ocean or near shores
Sea lion, walrus and seal
How they like fish for their meal
For they are flesh-eating water carnivores

UNGULATES - HOOFED MAMMALS

(to the tune of "Home on the Range")
Lyrics by Doug Eldon 1995

Two orders to know
You can tell by their toe
Having hoofs which can help them run well
They run on all fours
And they are herbivores
Known as ungulates or hoofed mammals

CHORUS #1
Oh, at home on the range
The grasslands where the hoofed mammals graze
When they run in a herd
They are much more secure
From becoming some carnivores' prey

The ungulates can
Be important to man
After years of domestication
They help to provide,
Clothes from their fur and hide
Meat, milk, and transportation

CHORUS #2
Oh, at home on the range
The grasslands where the hoofed mammals graze
They're cursorial,
Which means that they run well
To escape being carnivores' prey

The zebra and horse
And the donkey of course
One-toed animals no one forgets
The kinds with three toes
The tapirs and rhinos
Are the odd-numbered toed ungulates

CHORUS #1

The order that's left
All have hoofs that are cleft
Two or four toes and there's many kinds
Sheep, cattle and goat
Pronghorn, elk, antelope
Giraffe, camel, deer, hippo, and swine

The difference between
Horns and antlers is seen
Every year when the antlers are shed
For horns do not fall
But are part of the skull
And remain on the animal's head

CHORUS #2

PRIMATES
(to the tune of "Abraham's Daughters" or "Raw Recruits")
By Dorry and Doug Eldon 1995

Oh,we primates are the mammals that have five fingers and five toes
Opposing thumbs help us to grasp on to the things that we hold

Chorus:
We have large eyes, they all face front that help us, just for instance
To judge the depth of things close by and things off in the distance.
To judge the depth of things close by and things off in the distance.

There are fourteen families of us in this whole primate order
Lesser and great ape, two marmosets, the loris and the tarsier
Chorus

Three lemurs and the aye aye and the New and Old World monkeys
The human being but don't forget the so unusual Indris.
Chorus

Humans have large heads that hold big brains we use to our advantage
For problem solving, making tools, the oral and the written language
Chorus

RODENTS - GNAWING MAMMALS
(to the tune of "The E-ri-e")
by Dorry Eldon 1995

Squirrel, rat and porcupine
Rodents are the gnawing kind
There's lots of places where we find
Mammals of the gnawing kind
They move their jaw from front to back
As they chew their food attack
Incisor teeth that always grow
They must gnaw to keep them so low

Chorus:
They are mammals very small
They are the most numerous of all
There's about one thousand six hundred ninty species
Porcupine, squirrel, and rat-like, are suborders among these

They've got a space behind their incisor teeth
Some have pouches in their cheeks
But they grind with their cheek teeth
Beavers they can change a creek
Chisel teeth they use to bite
On our crops they are blight
Quickly multiply, a fright
Nocturnal some move at night
Chorus

Porcupine-like include nutria
Capybara and chinchilla
Rat-like are most rats and mice
Hamsters, lemmings, and the dormice
Squirrel-like are the prairie dog,
Chipmunk, beaver and groundhog
Squirrels of course and gophers too
Mice: only pocket and kangaroo
Chorus

RODENT-LIKE MAMMALS
(to the tune of "Irish Washerwoman")
by Dorry Eldon 1995

The rodent-like mammals include these two families
Hares with the rabbits, and pikas called conies
These mammals can move their jaws from side and side
And on most continents now they abide

Chorus:
The similar genera creates confusion
The hares are long-legged and born with eyes open
And rabbits are running, the short-legged kind
Their babies born furless with eyes that are blind

They've four incisor teeth on jaws that are upper
The hare is the species that is a high jumper
The family of pikas are animals small
They have short, broad ears and no tails at all
Chorus

All lagomorphs eat in herbivorous habit
The hares have long ears and include the jackrabbit
And rabbits include those whose tails are small:
The domestic rabbit and cottontails all
Chorus

BATS
(to the tune of "Take Me Out to the Ball Game")
by Dorry Eldon 1995

Bats are the flying mammals features designed for flight
Chiroptera is the order's name
Refers to the hands covered with flight membranes
That allow the bats to fly slowly and quickly dart in the sky
To catch flies, eat insects in the dark night as they fly

Nearly a thousand species and bats can navigate well
Most use a method that's like radar
Echolocation to know where things are
For they can squeak very high pitches that bounce off the objects nearby
And return to them as an echo as they fly

Bats disperse seeds of fruit trees, others pollinate plants
Insect control to the humans give
Bats return at dawn to the places they live
In the caves or up in the treetops to hang upside down by their feet
And the bats are really so helpful to man and beast

INSECTIVORES

(to the tune of "Camptown Races")
Lyrics by Dorry Eldon 1995

Insectivores are also called the insect-eaters
They include hedgehog and shrew, and solenodon too.
There's six families, four hundred six species
With tenrec and the golden mole, also the "true" mole

Here's some common traits among these insect-eaters:
Good sense of smell is what you'll find with species of this kind
Their eyes can be so small, not much use at all
And with their snouts so long and thin the ground they burrow in

A hedgehog's not a porcupine but an insect-eater
It is not hard to define, it has barbless spines
Most roll into a ball, if afraid at all
The porcupine so large and fat cannot roll up like that

The smallest mammal that is found is an insect-eater
It is called the pygmy shrew; they can eat meat too
Some can eat their weight in food every day
But elephant shrew and tree shrew have their own orders too

"TOOTHLESS" MAMMALS

(to the tune of "Yellow Rose of Texas")
by Dorry Eldon 1995

Armadillos live in Texas, south of the border too
Considered "toothless" mammals, anteater and sloth too
The anteater eats insects and worms found in the ground
The sloth likes to hang on the trees and view things upside down

The order's edentata, with creatures so diverse
Of course they are all mammals 'cause their babies, mothers nurse
Because the sloth lives in the trees, it is arboreal
Armadillos 'n anteaters that live on the land are terrestrial

The anteater's mouth is but a small hole of pencil size
Its sense of smell is keen cause it can't rely on its eyes
It finds an ant nest digs a bit and then inserts its snout
It uses its long sticky tongue to pull the insects out

Armadillos can defend themselves by their protective plates
That are skin-covered bone, this is the armadillo's trait
The tree sloth climbs from limb to limb its movement is so slow
But it can hardly walk at all if on the ground below

WHALES
CETACEANS
(to the tune of "Kingdom Coming")
Lyrics by Dorry Eldon 1995

These water mammals live in the ocean with the sharks and fish and rays
The six rorquals have throat grooves but not the bowhead, or the right, or gray
The whales are grouped according to their food and how they eat
These have baleen, they eat the plankton and those with sharp teeth eat meat

Chorus:
Cetaceans all have lungs, thou' live out in the sea
These mammals must all rise to the surface for they need the air to breathe

The whale has two flukes that together make a horizontal tail
It's powerful and it is so muscular it helps propel the whale
The largest of all living animals is the enormous blue
And with the right it has been hunted until now there's just a few
Chorus

Toothed whales include beluga, dolphin, and the sperm and the porpoise too
The orcas are the killer whales that together hunt the ocean blue
Baleen humpbacks leap high from the water and they also sing a song
They sing through their blowholes to other whales as they all swim along
Chorus

SIRENIANS
SEA COW, DUGONG AND MANATEE
(to the tune of "What Shall We do with a Drunken Sailor")
Lyrics by Dorry Eldon 1995

This order has two families
Sea cow or dugong, and manatee
They live in rivers, coastal seas
On only water plants they feed

Chorus:
Slow—ly moving mammals
Hea—vy bodied mammals
Such unique animals
Herbivorous water mammals

The order is Sirenian
Their bodies, heavy but they swim
With two flippers, but they don't have fins
They may walk the water floor with them
Chorus

Sailors thought they looked like mermaids
So they named them for those sirens
Drawing all to shores nearby them
In salt or fresh water they swim
Chorus

SINGLE-FAMILY ORDERS

(to the tune of "Should Old Acquaintance be Forgot")
by Dorry Eldon 1995

These mammals are the orders that have only one family
Combining them all in this song finishes mammal study
These mammals have little in common this I must repeat
They're single family orders that have 4 legs and 4 feet.

The elephants have ivory tusks and massive body size.
The trunks make eating easier because they can reach up high
The Asian is one type of two kinds of the elephant
The African has larger ears shaped like that continent

The pangolin is also called the scaly anteater
Protective coated plates help to defend this strange creature
The aardvark is a creature rare it has long ears and snout
It puts it into termite nests and then it pulls them out

The flying lemur looks like a bat but it can't really fly
It leaps from tree to treetop as along the air it glides
The hyraxes look like rodents except for their front teeth
Spaced triangular incisors; and they've sweat pads on their feet

Just recently the elephant shrew; also the tree shrew
Have been reclassified now each has its own order too.
Don't let these mammals be forgot, hold them in your mem'ry
As orders that are special 'cause they have just one family

ECOLOGY

(to the tune of "Sweet Betsy From Pike")
Lyrics by Doug Eldon 1995

Ecology is scientific study
Of relationships and interactions, you see,
Of living things one with another as well
As with their environment, where they all dwell
Singing ecolo-gy colo-gy cology

The living and nonliving environment
Are factors which are all interdependent
A community is all the organisms
That live together in an ecosystem
Singing ecolo-gy colo-gy cology

A group of the same kind of living thing
In the same area is the population
The number that's found of that single species
Is known as the population density
Singing ecolo-gy colo-gy cology

A habitat is a place where it is good
For a living thing to find its shelter and food
But the way that it lives and the things that it does
Creates the particular niche that it has
Singing ecolo-gy cology cology

Relationships include competition
The struggle with others in ecosystems
And with the environment to stay alive
Competing for the basic needs to survive
Singing ecolo-gy colo-gy cology

Predation is predators killing what they
Will then consume which is known as their prey
This relationship doesn't just benefit one
For predators help control populations
Singing ecolo-gy colo-gy cology

Living together is symbiosis
Where one or more organisms benefit
Commensal helps one, mutual helps them both
Parasites benefit at expense of their hosts
Singing ecolo-gy colo-gy cology

ECOLOGY PART 2

(to the tune of The Campbells are Coming)
Lyrics by Doug Eldon 1995

Plants make the food and they are producers
Animals that eat them are consumers
Eaters of dead things are scavengers
Bacteria-and fungi are decomposers

Chorus:
Ecologic'ly the energy flows
Round and again the cycle goes
From the sun to autotrophs
To interdependent heterotrophs

The plant-eaters are the herbivores
The meat-eaters are the carnivores
If they eat both then they're omnivores
And that is what you and I are, of course
Chorus

Falling water is precipitation
Liquid to gas is evaporation
Which from a plant leaf is transpiration
And turning back to clouds is condensation
Chorus

There're cycles involving nitrogen
Carbon dioxide and oxygen
Loose in the atmosphere and then
In soil, plants, animals and back again
Chorus

BIOMES

(to the tune of "Get Along Little Dogies" or "Whoopy Ti Yi Yo")
By Doug Eldon

Deserts are dry but the temperature varies
Tundras are dry, but all year it may freeze
Grasslands get more rain and may be called prairies
Savannas are grasslands that also have trees.

Chorus:
 Oh the biomes are regions with similar climate
(precipitation and temperatures)
 The climate determines soil and vegetation
Which then determines the kinds of creatures

In coniferous forests there are conifer trees
Needleleaf evergreens like pine and fir
Deciduous forests have trees that drop broad leaves
Rainforests are wet and warm most of the year
Chorus

The freshwater biome includes streams and rivers
Lakes, ponds, swamps, marshes, and lands that are wet
The saltwater biome, the seas and the oceans
Called the marine it's too large to forget
Chorus

NOTES

[1] Rue, Leonard Lee III. *Meet the Opossum*, Dodd, Mead and Company, New York, 1983. p.19–21.

[2] Nowak, Ronald M. and Paradiso, John L. *Walker's Mammals of the World 4th Edition,* Johns Hopkins University Press, Baltimore,1983. p.571–679.

[3] Vaughan, Terry, *Mammalogy*, W. B. Saunders Company, Philadelphia, 1972. p.144.

[4] Bat Conservation International, *Amazing Bat Trivia*, pamphlet 1993.

[5] Bat Conservation International, *Amazing Bat Trivia*, pamphlet 1993.

[6] Nowak and Paradiso, p.131.

[7] Barner, Bob, *Elephant Facts*, A Unicorn Book E.P. Dutton, New York, 1979. p.22.

[8] Barner, Bob, p.16.

FOR MORE INFORMATION...

We hope you enjoyed learning and singing about mammals! Of course, we could not mention them all, nor all the wonderful things about them—that takes volumes! If you want to know more please write to an organization listed below. They are eager to share information about their favorite mammal, and their careers with them.

For more information about these mammals

Bat Conservation International
P. O. Box 162603
Austin, Texas 78716
PH:1-800 538-BATS

Save the Manatee Club
500N. Maitland Ave.
Maitland, Florida
PH: 407 539-0990

Gorilla Foundation
P.O. Box 620-530
Woodside, CA 94062
PH: 1-800 63GOAPE

Wildlife Conservation Program
School of Forestry
University of Montana
Missoula, Montana 59812

Dr. Charles Jonkel, Scientific advisor
Great Bear Foundation
P.O. Box 9380
Missoula, Montana 59807
PH: 406 721-3009

Education Department
Dolphin Research Center
P.O. Box 522875
Marathon Shores, Florida 33052

For career information

Education and Human Resource Director
American Association for the Advancement
    of Science
1333 H. St. NW
Washington, D.C. 90560

Public Relations
American Veterinary Medical Association
1931 N. Meacham Rd. Suite 100
Schaumburg, Illinois 60173 - 4360

Dr. Pat Nellor Wickwire
American Association for Career Education
2900 Amby Place
Hermosa Beach, CA 90254-2216
Your request will be forwarded to a member
in the particular science field requested.

BIBLIOGRAPHY

Anderson, Margaret J., *Food Chains The Unending Cycle*, Enslow Publishers, New Jersey, 1991.

Arnold, Caroline, *Koala,* William Morrow and Company Inc., New York,1987.

Barner, Bob, *Elephant Facts*, A Unicorn Book E. P. Dutton, New York, 1979.

Boorer, Michael, *Mammals of the Worl,.* Grosset and Dunlap, New York ,1971.

Breeden, Stanley and Kay, *The Life of the Kangaroo*, Taplinger Publishing Co., New York, 1966.

Cadbury, B. Bartram, *Fresh and Salt Water*, Creative Educational Society, Minnesota, 1967.

Darling, Kathy, *Manatee on Location,* Lothrop, Lee, and Shepard Books, New York, 1991.

Ganeri, Anita, *The Usborne Book of Animal Facts*, Usborne Publishing, London, 1988.

Jenkins, Marie, *Goats, Sheep and How They Live*, Holiday House, New York, 1978.

Lavine, Sigmund, *Wonders of Rhinos*, Dodd, Mead and Company, New York, 1982.

McClung, Robert, *Hunted Mammals of the Sea*, William Morrow and Company, New York, 1978.

National Geographic, *Book of Mammals Volume One and Two*, National Geographic Society, Washington, D.C., 1981.

Nickelsburg, Janet, *Ecology*, J. B. Lippincott, Philadelphia, 1969.

Nowak, Ronald M. and Paradiso, John L., *Walker's Mammals of the World 4th Edition,* Johns Hopkins University Press, Baltimore and London, 1983.

Papatavrou, Vassili, *Eyewitness Books, Whale*, Alfred A. Knopf, New York, 1993.

Pembleton, Seliesa, *The Armadillo*, Dillion Press, New York, 1992.

Pringle, Laurence, *Ecology Science of Survival*, Macmillan Company, New York, 1971.

Reid, Keith, *Nature's Network*, Natural History Press, Garden City, New York, 1970.

Ricciuti, Edward R., *What on Earth is a Pangolin*, Blackbirch Press , Woodbride, Connecticut, 1994.

Rue, Leonard Lee III, *Meet the Opossum*, Dodd, Mead and Company, New York, 1983.

Sandburg, Carl, *The American Songbag*, Harcourt, Brace and Company, New York, 1927.

Scuro, Vincent, *Wonders of Cattle*, Dodd, Mead and Company, New York, 1980.

Sibler, Irwin, *Songs of the Great Americn West.* MacMillan company, New York, 1967.

Stuart, Dee, *Bats Mysterious Flyers of the Night*, Carolrhoda Books, Minneapolis, 1994.

Vaughan, Terry, *Mammalogy*, W. B. Saunders Company, Philadelphia, 1972.

Zim, Herbert S. and Hoffmeister, Donald F., *Mammals a Guide to Familiar American Species* Revised Edition, Golden Press, New York, 1987.

INDEX

A
aardvark 75
aardwolves 19
abiotic factors 79
alpaca 30
anteater 62
antelope 33, 34
apes 40, 41
aquatic 7
arboreal 7
arid 88
armadillos 61
ass 26
autotroph 82
aye aye 39

B
baboon 4
Bactrian 30
backbone 5
badgers 19
baleen 6, 66
baleen whales 65, 67
bats 53-55
bears 18
beavers 45
belugas 67
biodiversity 93
biotic factors 79
bison 33
blubber 5, 65
blue whale 65 ,66
bovine 33–35
bowhead 65
brachiators 7
browsers 10, 34
buffalo 33

C
camel 30
canid 18
canine 6, 17
canopy 92
capybara 47
caprine 35
carbohydrates 82
carnassials 6, 17
carnivore 6, 17-20, 82
carrion 19, 62
cats 20
cattle 33
cetaceans 65, 67
chaparral 92
cheek pouches 14, 43
chevrotain 32

chickarees 44
chimpanzees 41
chinchillas 47
classification 6
climate 87
clinger-leapers 7, 38
chipmunks 44
commensal 80
community 79
condensation 83
coniferous forests 91
consumers 6, 82
coyotes 18
cud 29
cursorial 7, 25

D
deciduous forest 91
decomposers 82
deer 32
desert 88
diurnal 44
diastema 43, 49
dogs 18
dolphin 67
donkey 25
dormice 47
dromedary 30
duck-billed platypus 14
dugong 69–71

E
eared seals 21
echidna 15
echolocation 54, 58
ecology 79
ecosystem 79
ectothermic 5
edentata 61-63
egg-laying mammals 6
elephant 73
elephant shrews 76
endothermic 5
energy cycles 82, 83
environment 79
environmental factors 79
equines 25
estuaries 95
evaporation 83

F
felines 20
filter feeders 66
flying foxes 54
flying lemur 75

food chain 82
food web 82
foxes 18
freshwater biome 94

G
gestation 9
gibbon 41
giraffe 32
goat 33, 35
Goeldi's marmoset 39
golden mole 57, 59
gopher 44
gorilla 41
grassland 89
gray whale 66
grazers 10, 34
grazing herbivores 10
great apes 41
ground hogs 44
guanaco 3

H
hamsters 46
habitat 79
hare 50
hedgehog 57, 58
herbivores 6, 82
heterotrophs 82
hippopotamus 30
homo sapiens 37, 41
hoofed mammals 25
horse 25
humpback whale 66
hyena 19
hyrax 76

I
Insectivores 57, 58
incisors 6
indigenous 49
indri 38
interdependent 79
intertidal 95

J
jackals 18

K
kangaroo 9
kangaroo rats 45
killer whales 67
koala 11
krill 65

L
lagomorpha 49
lemmings 46
lemur 38
lesser ape 41
llamas 30
loris 37

M
mammary glands 5
manatee 69–71
marine 7
marine biome 95
marmoset 39
marmots 44
marsupials 9
marsupium 9
megachiropterans 54
mice 46
microchiroptera 54
migrate 34
molars 6, 17
moles 57–59
mongoose 19
monotremes 9, 13
mountain beavers 45
mouse deer 32
muskrats 47

N
narwhals 67
New World bats 54
New World monkeys 40
New World porcupines 47
nocturnal 11
non-selective eaters 10

O
okapi 32
Old World bats 54
Old World monkey 40
omnivore 6, 82
opossum 12
orangutan 41
orca 67
otter 19

P
pangolin 74
pikas 49
parasitic 80
parasitoid 80
peccaries 29
pelage 5
permafrost 88
photosynthesis 82

pigs 29
pinnipeds 21
placenta 6
placental mammals 6
plankton 65
platypus 14
pods 66
pocket mice 45
polar biome 89
population 79
population density 79
porcupine-like rodents 47
porpoise 67
pouched mammals 6
prairie 89
prairie dogs 44
precipitation 83
predation 80
predator 80
predominance 22
prehensile 37
premolars 6, 17
primate 37
producers 6, 82
pronghorn 33
pygmy shrew 58–59

R
rabbit 50
raccoons 18
rainforest 92, 93
rat-like rodent 46
rats 46
reproduction 6
respiration 82
retract 20
rhinoceros 28
right whale 66
riparian 94
rodents 43, 43–45
rorquals 66
ruminants 29, 31–32

S
savannas 90
scaly anteater 74
scavengers 82
sea lions 21
sea cow 69–71
seals 21
semiaquatic 38
sewellel 45
sheep 33, 35
shrews 57, 58
sifaka 38
sirenians 69–71

skunks 19
sloths 63
solenodons 57, 58
sperm whale 67
spiny anteater 15
squirrel 44
squirrel-like rodents 44, 45
steppes 89
survival of the fittest 80

T
tamarin 39
tapir 27
tarsier 39
tenrecs 57, 58
terrestrial 7
tetrapods 7
timberline 89
toothed whales 65
transpiration 83
tree shrew 77
tundra 88

U
ungulates 25

V
vegetation 87
velvet 32
vertebrae 5
vicuna 30
voles 46

W
walrus 21
warmblooded 5
water cycle 83
weasels 19
whalebone 66
whales 65–6
wolverines 19
wolves 18
wombat 11
woodchucks 44

X
xenarthrale 61

Z
zebra 25
zooplankton 65